Beverly Hills

PORTRAIT OF A FABLED CITY

Beverly Hills

PORTRAIT OF A FABLED CITY

FRED E. BASTEN

Douglas-West Publishers
Los Angeles, California

Library of Congress Catalog Card Number: 75-22571
ISBN: 0-913264-23-7

Published by Douglas-West Publishers, Inc.
Los Angeles, California 90028

Printed in the United States of America

First Printing

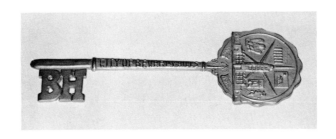

TO THE FRIENDS OF BEVERLY HILLS
without whose help
this book
never could have happened.

ILLUSTRATIONS

Portola Expedition Plaque, 9
First Families Arrive, 10
Canyon Stream, 12
Rodeo de las Aguas Plaque, 13
Historic Indian Raid Site, 14
Rodeos, 15
Famed Eucalyptus Tree, 16
Brands of the Ranchos, 17
Adobe, Hammel & Denker Ranch, 18-19
Lima Bean Fields, 20-21
Balloon Route, 22
Burton E. Green, 24-25
The First House, 27
Early Business Building, 28
Young Palms on Canon Drive, 29
Crescent Drive through an Arch, 30-31
The Beverly Hills Hotel, 32-33

The Main Entrance to the Hotel, 34
Hotel Hollywood, 35
Sunset Park, 36
Fountain in the Park, 37
Depot and Park, 38
Park Way Fountain, 39
The Lily Pond, 40-41
North Canon Drive, 42-43
North from Park Way, 44
Sunset Park Aerial, 45
Santa Monica Boulevard, 46
Burton Green Estate, 48
Kirk B. Johnson Estate, 49
Roland P. Bishop Residence, 50
Max Whittier Estate, 50-51
Beverly Hills Grammar School, 52
Hawthorne School, 53

Beverly Drive, 55
Beverly Hills Speedway, 56-61
Pickfair, 62-65
The Business District, 66-67
Pacific Electric Depot, 68-69
Stars for "Stagnation," 70-71
Memorial to Stars, 71
Ye Bridle Path, 72-73
Demonstration at Santa Monica & Wilshire, 74-75
Church of the Good Shepherd, 76-79
Aerial Views from South to North, 80-81
Residences of the Twenties 82-88
"Homes of the Stars" Tours, 89
Beverly Hills Women's Club, 90-91
Hunter and Hounds, 92-93
Beverly Vista School, 94-95
Horse Show, 96-99
Berkeley Hall School, 100-101
UCLA, 102-103
American Legion Post, 103
Beverly Hills Community Church, 104-107
All Saints' Episcopal Church, 108-111
Will Rogers "Elected" Mayor, 112-113
El Rodeo School, 114-115
Beverly Hills High School, 116-119
Tournament of Roses, 120-121
Municipal Water Plant, 122-123
Greystone Mansion, 126-133
Advertising of the Twenties, 134-135
South on Beverly Drive, 136-137
Greenacres, 138-151
Showplaces, 152-153

The Beverly Wilshire, 154-155
Beverly Hills Nursery, 156
Chamber of Commerce, 157
Chamber of Commerce Banquets, 158
Society Circus, 159
Horace Mann School, 160-161
Olympic and Beverly, 162-163
Wilshire Boulevard, 165
Beverly Drive Business District, 166-167
Christmas Nights, 168-169
Beverly Hills Catholic School, 170-171
Wilshire and Little Santa Monica, 172-173
The Brown Derby, 174-177
Beverly Gardens, 178-186
Coldwater Canyon Park, 186-187
LaCienega Park, 188-189
Roxbury Park, 190-191
Wilshire Boulevard, 192
Wilshire and Santa Monica, 193
City Hall, 194-195
Fire Department, 196
The Canyons of Beverly Hills, 198-199
The Beverly Hills Hotel, 200-203
The Post Office, 204-205
Beverly Hills National Bank, 206
Residences of the Thirties, 207-211
KMPC Radio, 212
Doheny and Olympic, 213
Beverly Hills Citizen, 214-215
First Church of Christ, Scientist, 216-217
Advertising of the Thirties, 218-219
Temple Emanuel, 220-225

Mt. Calvary Lutheran Church, 227
"City of Beverly Hills" Super Fortress, 228
Bond Drive Registration, 229
Residences of the Forties, 230-231
Wilshire at Hamilton Drive, 232-233
Business Establishments, 234-235
Beverly and Wilshire, 236-237
Mountaintop Radio Station, 238-239
Wilshire and Robertson, 240
Romanoff's, 241
The Beverly Hills Hotel, 242-245
North from Pico, 246-247
YMCA, 248
Beverly Hills Street Sign, 249
Will Rogers Park, 250-251
Robinson's Beverly, 252
Frank Lloyd Wright Building, 253
Beth Jacob Congregation, 254-255
Favored Establishments, 256
Wilshire at Night, 257
Restaurant Row, 258
Advertising of the Fifties, 259-261
Stars at "Golden" Premiere, 262-263
The Beverly Hilton, 264-269
Trousdale Estates, 270-283
Beverly Hills Police Department, 284-285
Beverly Hills High School, 286-287
The Beverly Wilshire Hotel, 288-289
Residences of the Fifties, 290-295
Rodeo Drive, 297
Anniversary Celebrations, 298-299
Residences of the Sixties, 300-305

Beverly Hills Public Library, 306-307
Wilshire at Canon, 308-309
Sunset Boulevard Residence, 309
Sister City Program, 310
The Building Boom, 312-313
The Shops of Beverly Hills, 314
The Beverly Rodeo Hotel, 315
The Friars Club, 316
Wilshire and Santa Monica, 317
The Beverly Hills Tennis Club, 318
Looking East Over Beverly Hills, 319
Wilshire and LaCienega, 320
William Morris Agency, 321
Litton Industries Plaza, 322-327
Gateway Lodge, 328
Sunset Boulevard, 329
Lexington Road, 330
Municipal Court, 331
The Beverly Wilshire Hotel, 332-337
Crescent Drive, 338
Beverly Drive, 339
Names and Places, 340-345
East on Sunset Boulevard, 346-347
The Beverly Hills Hotel, 348-353
Street Scene, 354-355
Residences of the Seventies, 356-361
Block Party, 362
Academy of Motion Picture Arts & Sciences, 363
Wilshire Boulevard, 364-365
The New Look, 366-373
El Rodeo de las Aguas, 374
Beverly Hills Panorama, 376-377

THE EARLY DAYS

Quiet, grassy plains topped with columns of sycamores; gently rolling hills stretching to the sea; soft ocean breezes and the warmth of a semitropical sun. The land had little to distinguish it from dozens of similar hill-hugging areas that lined the sweeping valley floor. But its destiny was to set it apart from all the others.

Into this serene setting, the site of the future Beverly Hills, stepped the first white explorers on the afternoon of August 3, 1769. They were members of a company of leather-jacketed soldiers, led by Captain Don Gaspar de Portola, Spanish Governor of the Californias. Following an Indian trail that is now Wilshire Boulevard, the party had worked its way from Mexico en route to found, in the name of the King of Spain, the

first settlements in the Province of Alta California.

Marching northward from the newly founded San Diego, where the group had left a cluster of travel-weary companions, including the saintly Father Junipero Serra, they had spent the previous evening camped on the banks of the River Porciúncula and had given to the place the name of El Pueblo de Nuestra Senora la Reina de Los Angeles de Porciúncula (the town of Our Lady the Queen of the Angels of Porciúncula), which soon became popularly known as El Pueblo and, in time, Los Angeles. At sunrise on August 3rd, they crossed the river and headed west, passing Indians along the way who "howled like wolves and proferred seeds as offerings." One village of native Californians was settled near the banks of the

Plaque commemorating the Portola Expedition was placed in LaCienega Park in 1959. It is a California Historical Landmark.

river, another about midway between the river and today's Beverly Hills, and a third nearer the bay in what is now West Los Angeles.

As they approached the region that was destined to become Beverly Hills, they discovered "a grove of very large sycamores, high and thick." From it flowed a stream of water "as deep as an ox" which ran toward the southwest between grassy banks covered with fragrant herbs and watercress. (They named the spot the "Spring of the Sycamores of St. Stephen;" histor-

ians believe it fed what is known today as La Ballona Creek.) An abundance of antelope and deer impressed Portola, while Father Juan Crespi, whose journal traced the expedition, wrote of "sweet springs surrounded by innumerable bushes of wild roses of Castile."

Following Portola's famous march through California, presidios, missions and pueblos were established and a wave of soldiers, priests and colonists came north from Mexico. It was a period of relative tranquility; even the

Maria Rita's family and future husband arrived in California from Mexico with the expeditions of 1781, a last-ditch stand to colonize Alta California. (Recreated by the Los Angeles Museum of Natural History.)

cession of California to the United States by the Treaty of Guadalupe Hidalgo in 1848, and its admission to the Union as a State in 1850, went generally unnoticed.

As colonists migrated to the new land, individuals whose names would be known longer than a lifetime were included among them. Eugenio Valdez, a soldier from Sonoma, his parents and young bride, arrived in 1781. That same year, a six-year-old boy named Vicente Ferrer Villa, came to California with his family and another group of settlers, traveling a different route from Sonoma on their way to San Gabriel.

Valdez and Villa would one day be linked with Beverly Hills' first settler and owner, Maria Rita Valdez. The soldier was her father. The young boy grew up to become her husband.

Exactly when Maria Rita Valdez and her soldier husband, who was serving as a corporal in the Santa Barbara Company, came to live in "Beverly Hills" is not known. It is estimated, however, to be about 1822, the year that Spanish rule gave way to Mexican. In 1828, José Antonio Carrillo, Alcalde (Mayor) of Los Angeles, recalled visiting the Villa family at their ranch on a boundary matter. The ranch had been named "Rodeo de las Aguas"—the gathering of the waters—

derived from the meeting of streams that in rainy months rushed from "Cañada de las Aguas Frias" (Coldwater Canyon) and "Cañada de los Encinos" (now Benedict Canyon), creating a chain of *cienegas* or swamps in the lower lands that extended across the plain. Not long after Carrillo's visit, Maria Rita was widowed, left with eleven children.

In 1831, a tract of land known as "San Antonio" was granted jointly to Maria Rita and a relative named Luciano Valdez. She now called the property by its legal name, dropping the adopted family name of Rodeo de las Aguas.

A home for Maria Rita and her children was built on the property, somewhere near the present northwest corner of Sunset Boulevard and Alpine Drive. She brought in cattle and horses and let them roam. She

cultivated a small garden. It seemed idyllic—but she was soon to discover that a 4,539-acre ranch was much too small for her family, particularly if one of the members was Luciano Valdez.

Luciano had constructed his home too close to Maria Rita's to suit her. He countered her complaints by refusing her cattle the only watering place on the ranch, leaving her herd to wander into the neighboring ranchos. The feuds became constant and more heated. It's said that Luciano was overly proud of his ability to read and write (he had been a schoolmaster for three years) and that he suffered from "bad temper" and was "intolerable."

Maria Rita's complaints were turned over to the Los Angeles City Council which promptly ordered Luciano to vacate the premises. The bickering continued, for

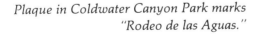

Plaque in Coldwater Canyon Park marks "Rodeo de las Aguas."

During the winter months, streams ran freely from the canyons, forming cienegas in the flatlands.

Historic Indian raid site, on the grounds of the Beverly Hills Women's Club, was marked by the Daughters of the American Revolution, Beverly Hills Chapter, in 1930.

Maria Rita had to pay Luciano for his share of the rancho. Appraisers set a value of fifteen dollars on his home, two dollars on a peach tree, and one-half dollar on "two poles for farming purposes." On August 11, 1844, Maria Rita paid Luciano a total of $17.50; the property was hers subject to final patent.

Indian raids, notably those by Chief Walker and his Utah band, were becoming more frequent. Maria Rita, who had been dividing her time between the rancho and her home in Los Angeles (located at the present site of Temple and Main Streets), was caught by surprise one day in 1852. Three Indians, hiding behind a sycamore tree at the rear of her adobe, opened fire. The attack lasted for several hours, until Maria Rita's ammunition began to run low. At that point, one of the younger family members slipped unnoticed from the house. Crawling in a shallow ditch for half a mile until clear enough to run free, he dashed to the town of Sherman (now West Hollywood) for help. Ranchers on horseback came to the rescue, chasing the Indians to a walnut grove near today's Chevy Chase and Benedict Canyon Drives where they shot and buried them.

By 1854, continuing unrest and problems at the rancho prompted Maria Rita to sell. A neighbor to the west, Benjamin Davis Wilson ("Don Benito"—a developer of Riverside, Pasadena, Alhambra, Westwood and for whom Mount Wilson was named) and Major Henry Hancock, whose family had bought Rancho LaBrea and its tar pits on the east, offered her $4000; $500 in cash, $500 in notes and the remainder to be paid when the United States confirmed the title. The two partners, with their combined ranches, hoped to turn their newly acquired land into a vast wheat field. But the team was short-lived. Hancock, notoriously land poor, was forced to sell his share of the rancho to another American, William Workman.

By the early 1860s, the new duo had planted 2,000 acres in wheat, erected a long three-room ranch house, and, to protect the anticipated bumper crop from roaming cattle (over 78,000 head roamed Los Angeles County), walled in the property on all but the mountain side with an expensive four-board fence. It seemed they couldn't miss in their new venture.

Problems, the nemesis of Maria Rita, were to plague Wilson and Workman as well. Vandals, squatters and rancheros, dismantled their fence piece by piece. Drought withered their crops, erased the gathering waters and hardened the land. Herds of cattle were without food or drink; ranchers, unable to feed or sell their cattle, were forced to drive entire herds from the Palos Verdes cliffs into the sea. The dry years of 1863

Until the parching drought of the 1860s, cattle roamed at will across the open land. Twice-yearly rodeos were held to separate the stock and mark the calves with the owners' brands.

and 1864 took their toll, not only in the future Beverly Hills but across the basin. Fortunes were lost, banks closed, panic was widespread. When the rains finally returned, they too were in extreme. The caked land could not accept the deluge. Water roared down the canyons, rivers overflowed, and the flatlands became a massive lake.

It took something as big as oil to renew the spirit of the people. In 1865, news came from Santa Barbara that prospecting was certain, based on geologists' predictions of petroleum deposits. The Pioneer Oil Company was organized in Los Angeles and began buying oil rights, among the first being those to Rancho Rodeo de las Aguas. Investors felt that its proximity to Rancho LaBrea, with its great surface slicks, assured production. Officers of the new company included "Don Benito" Wilson, Phineas Banning and Governor John G. Downey. Enthusiasm was so high it seemed all a salesman needed to do to sell stock was "rub a little tar on his sleeve and talk of barrels and wells." And while a "strike" was recorded near the north end of the rancho, the effort proved premature.

Opposite page: for years, cattle roundups were centered around this famous eucalyptus. Located just north of Pico Boulevard off Preuss Road (now Robertson Boulevard) on the Whitworth Ranch, it became a center of controversy in the 1920s. Road-widening and falling branches (nurserymen nicknamed the specie "widow makers") doomed it, even though Cecil B. DeMille and other notables offered to purchase and present it to the city rather than see it cut down.

BRANDS OF THE RANCHOS

Mariano Villa

José Antonio Rocha
of Rancho La Brea

Maria Rita Valdez de Villa

Benjamin Davis Wilson

Domingo Amestoy

Edward A. Preuss

Remi Nadeau

Hammel & Denker

As interest in oil declined, a new word became popular: wool. Sheep suddenly were as numerous on the rancho as cattle had once been. Domingo Amestoy and Bernart Domaleche, enterprising Basque sheepherders, purchased 160 acres of "Don Benito's" land for $500. Amestoy alone, within the next ten years, would accumulate an estimated 30,000 head of sheep—and a fortune.

Soon others appeared to farm and to raise sheep. James Whitworth bought 125 acres for $1,150 in the area north of the present Pico Boulevard (between Robertson and LaCienega Boulevards). Until labeled a hazard, a giant eucalyptus tree stood on Robertson near Pico, a monument to the Whitworth Ranch.

Another newcomer was Edson A. Benedict, a Los Angeles storekeeper from Missouri. At the mouth of the now Benedict Canyon, he built his home. His son, Pierce, followed and acquired the adjoining land. Together they planted walnut trees, beans and other vegetables, and raised bees. That same year, 1868, a German pharmacist and wool dealer from Louisville, Dr. Edward A. Preuss, purchased the remaining acreage of the rancho—3,608 acres for $10,775. The following year, the enterprising Dr. Preuss, who be-

The adobe shown on these pages was one of three located on the Hammel & Denker Ranch. Known as "the Antonio Roches adobe," it is not known who built it or when. The old buildings were removed with the laying out and development of Beverly Hills.

20

Looking south along rows of lima beans on the Hammel & Denker Ranch, ca 1900.

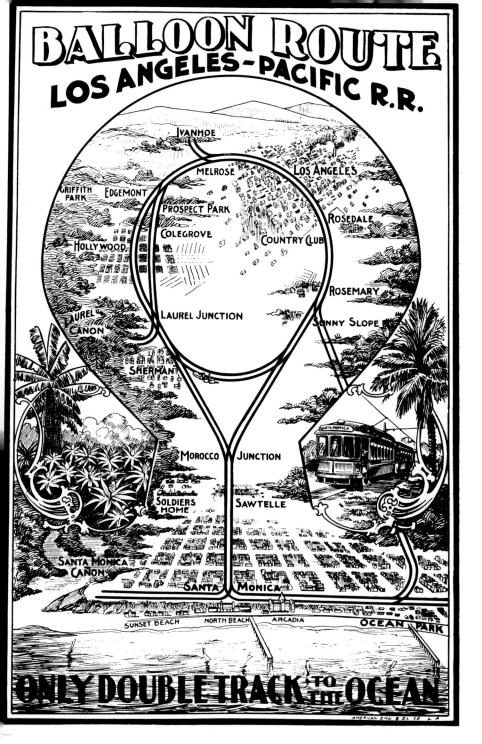

came one of the first presidents of the Los Angeles Athletic Club as well as Postmaster of Los Angeles, sold Francis P.F. Temple half of his interest. In turn, the two men deeded their land to the De Las Aguas Land Association, organized for subdivision purposes. The price: $32,000.

Nearly the entire ranch was divided into 75-acre farm lots, with the center reserved for the "Town of Santa Maria"—designed with large blocks, spacious lots (priced at $10 each) and wide streets running in each direction. One was named "Los Angeles Avenue" (now Wilshire Boulevard). Others, such as Adelphina, Caroline, Minna and Josephine, faded along with the flegling German colony itself. Once again drought was responsible for the failure. "Santa Maria" returned to its rancho status and bands of sheep reappeared, this time belonging to Remi Nadeau, the colorful French Canadian who was accumulating masses of money by transporting ore from the Panamint mines across the desert to Los Angeles with his twenty-mule-team wagons.

In the 1880s, the rancho began to be acquired, parcel by parcel, by Charles Denker and Henry Hammel, managers of the elegant and prosperous United States Hotel (where "every bed was a spring bed") at Main and Market Streets in Los Angeles. To their thinking,

Morocco Junction (now Beverly Hills) was a crossroads on the old "Balloon Route." Ad from 1902.

the land would be best used as a supply center for products consumed at the hotel. At one point, the ranch appeared to be "one vast field of lima beans."

The Hammel & Denker Ranch, as it became known, soon grew into a country settlement of sorts. Children were born and raised in the farm houses that dotted the land, awed by the development that seemed to be taking place in the outlying areas that all but surrounded them. A highlight of their days, reportedly, was watching the steam train as it traveled on unballasted tracks across the ranch, carrying passengers from Los Angeles to the popular North Beach in Santa Monica.

The land boom of the late 1880s was on. Easterners flocked to Southern California in search of The Golden Land. New towns appeared like wildflowers. The "townsite of Cahuenga" (now the Hollywood area) made headlines as did "Sunset" (today's Westwood) and "LaBallona" (Marina del Rey). Even a spot just off the continually expanding Hammel & Denker Ranch received attention. Called "Morocco," it was an imaginary town that consisted of no more than a tiny train depot. Morocco itself never materialized. Its life, in fact, was so short it never reached the County Recorder. Most of the other overnight towns suffered similar fates in the collapse of the big boom.

Around 1890 the Coldwater School District was formed and a school opened in a little frame building at the entrance to Coldwater Canyon. (The first school established in what is now Beverly Hills is said to have opened in 1877. It was located just east of Doheny Drive and south of Sunset Boulevard.) The one-room Coldwater School House, as it was known, boasted "a few well-thumbed books, a cast-iron stove, and a drinking pail at the rear of the room." Its pupils came on horseback and in buggies from miles around to be taught by teachers who took turns living with different residents a few weeks at a time. Life on the farm continued at its even, steady pace. No one even suspected that a drastic change was about to take place.

"Black gold" once again triggered interest in the ranch lands. In 1900, spearheaded by a wealthy group of businessmen, including Burton E. Green, Charles A. Canfield, Max Whittier and W.G. Kerckhoff, the Amalgamated Oil Company purchased the Hammel & Denker holdings for development. Like the first venture 35 years before, it proved a failure. Amalgamated's equipment was unable to drill deep enough to tap the supply. Unlike the first venture, the land did not remain idle. In place of oil, the new owners had struck water. The Rodeo Land and Water Company was born.

THE MAN BEHIND THE DREAM

Burton E. Green was born on the outskirts of Madison, Wisconsin, on September 6, 1868. His early education in public schools and at Beaver Dam Academy in his native state served him well, stimulating his interest in learning and life.

At 16, he moved with his family to California and continued his education. It wasn't too long, however, before the infant oil industry had captured his attention. In time, he became one of the founders of the Associated Oil Company of California and, later, the president of Bellridge Oil in Kern County.

The founding of Beverly Hills was his greatest achievement and proudest accomplishment. Aside from his family, his city and magnificent estate on Lexington Road were his greatest joys. Unlike most pioneers, Burton Green lived to see his dreams come true. Active virtually all of his distinguished life, he died at age 96 in 1965.

Mr. Green was married to Lilian Wellborn, the daughter of Judge Olin Wellborn. They had three daughters: Dorothy (Dolly), Liliore and Burton, named after her father.

A CITY BEGINS

Guided by its president, Burton E. Green, the new corporation was dedicated to found a residential community second to none—one with broad tree-lined streets, spacious lots and generous parks. Expert engineers and landscaping specialists were hired; Wilbur Cook, a prominent landscape architect from New York was appointed to create the master plan.

The community was given a new name. "Beverly" was chosen after "Beverly Farms" in Massachusetts, a spot Mr. Green fondly remembered. "Hills" was selected in recognition of the landscape.

On January 23, 1907, the subdivision was officially recorded. Gently curving streets, lavishly bordered with palm trees, acacias and peppers, were christened Rodeo, Cañon, Crescent and Beverly Drives. Between them, running east and west, were planned Park Way, Carmelita, Elevado and Lomitas. Necessary improve-

ments were provided and, at great expense, telephone connections with Los Angeles were secured. Visitors were invited to see this planned model community, accessible by streetcar, then running hourly, or by private means via Santa Monica, West Adams or Wilshire Boulevards.

One such visitor who, in 1907 responded to an ad in the Los Angeles papers recalled, "We got off the Pacific Electric car at the station and looked around. Very young trees, uniform in variety and spacing, had a sort of merry, hopeful look. Four or five so-called 'company' houses were under construction . . . and a large English-type, two-story frame and stucco building was being erected on the southwest corner of Beverly Drive and Burton Way (now Little Santa Monica Boulevard). Its purpose was to house a general store, a post office and, upstairs, a recreation hall. South of the tracks there were three north-south streets: Cañon, Beverly and Rodeo, ending at Wilshire. The streets were well-

In 1907, Henry C. Clark built the first house in Beverly Hills, located on Crescent Drive near Lomitas. In those days, residential lots south of Sunset Boulevard were priced at $1,000 with a ten percent discount for cash (and another ten percent if improved within six months). But luxury was hardly the word then. Street lights, gas and sewers were still months away. And the winds rolling across the open spaces discouraged many a visitor from "staking a claim."

A visitor recalled seeing "an English-type, two-story frame and stucco building" under construction in 1907.

paved with the exception of Sunset, Santa Monica and Wilshire which merely had a 20-foot strip of oil and macadam in the center."

The transformation within Beverly Hills created little stir outside its borders. By 1910, less than six new permanent resident houses had been built north of Santa Monica Boulevard. Obviously, daring new promotional efforts were necessary. They took shape that same year as a magnificent new structure began rising at the base of the foothills. It was called the Beverly Hills Hotel.

Young palms follow curving borders of Cañon Drive; looking north.

THE BIG GAMBLE

Standing like a fortress in the midst of tilled fields, the Beverly Hills Hotel looked strangely out of place. But it did create a grand sight, its noble Spanish architecture spread beneath the rolling ridges of the Santa Monica Mountains.

The decision of the Rodeo Land and Water Company to build the hotel appeared to be a monumental gamble. Nor was it any less a gamble for Mrs. Margaret Anderson, then manager of the highly successful Hotel Hollywood, when she was approached to leave her secure position in town for the unknown in "the wilds." Against the advice of her friends and

associates, she accepted the job—as well as a chance to buy the hotel, which she eventually did. Mrs. Anderson did not come to her new position unprepared. She brought along her staff, many of the furnishings and, because of her renowned reputation, a number of clients from the Hotel Hollywood.

The Beverly Hills Hotel, with its picturesque bungalows, lush lawns and gardens, became an immediate success and soon established an international reputation. Winters found the hotel packed with guests from the larger cities of the Midwest and East, many of whom could not be persuaded to return to their homes. More and more retired and active businessmen arrived, not only to stay and establish homes but businesses as well.

The gamble had worked. Beverly Hills was on its way.

Looking east across Crescent Drive through an arch in the east portico of the Beverly Hills Hotel, ca 1912.

The main entrance to the Beverly Hills Hotel, ca 1912.

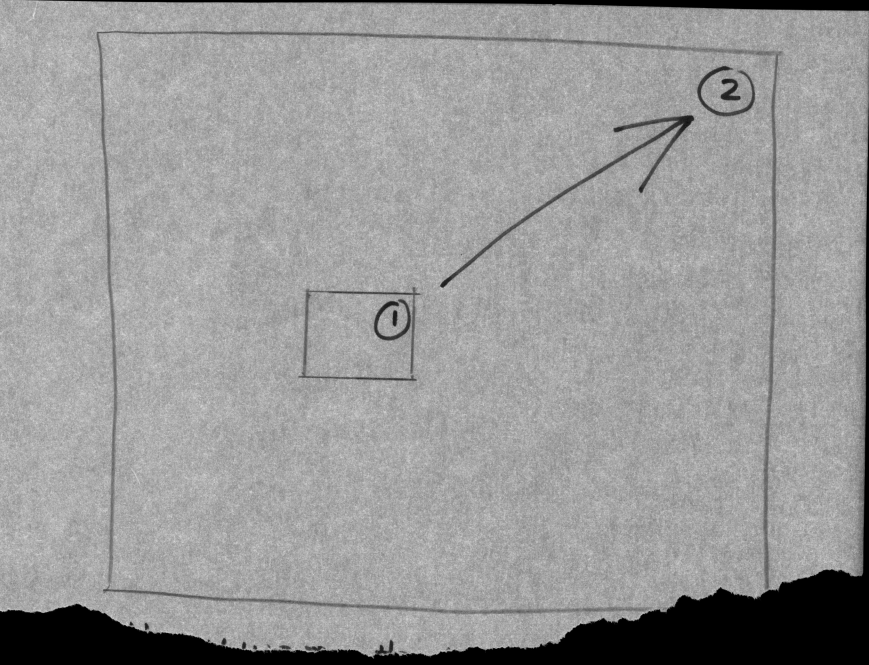

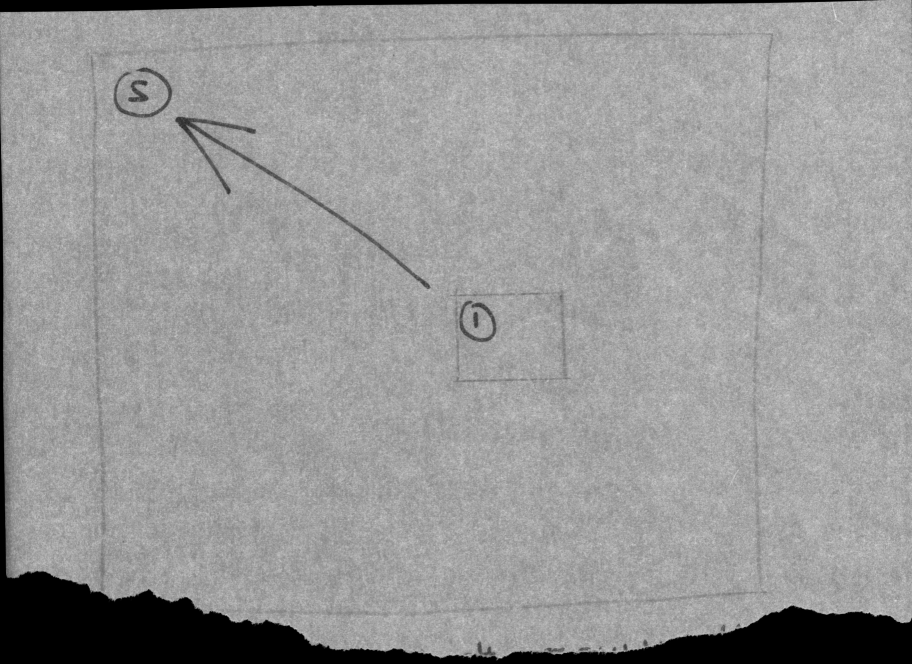

The thriving Hotel Hollywood in Hollywood lost Mrs. Margaret Anderson and many of its prized residents to the new hotel in Beverly Hills.

Fountain in the park, 1950s.

The terraced triangle of flower gardens, pools and shady walkways at the foot of the Beverly Hills Hotel was originally landscaped as part of the hotel grounds. In contrast to the stark, surrounding fields, the striking apron of color made quite an impression on newcomers. Ca 1915.

37

DIAMOND
IN THE ROUGH

With most potential buyers arriving at the Pacific Electric Depot, at best a lonely outpost in the "wilderness," their first impression had to be positive. As a sales gimmick, a park was decided upon, and a three block stretch along Santa Monica Boulevard, from Crescent to Rodeo, was developed with spacious grassy areas, trees and other plantings, and a massive lily pond. And so there would be no mistake that they had indeed made it to the promised land, a huge arched sign contained the twelve letters, BEVERLY HILLS.

Lushly landscaped park across from depot helped detract visitors' eyes from the stark surroundings. Fountain (right photo) overlooked Park Way.

The town now had two lovely parks. And while many more acres were committed for park development in the original master plan, no one would ever have believed in 1912 that it would be nearly 20 years before new parklands would be created.

The Beverly Hills sign, arched and vine covered, and the colorful lily pond were trademarks for nearly sixty years. Today, the sign is gone and the pond is planted with "earth flowers."

A NEW SPIRIT

With the prestige of the hotel, Beverly Hills took on new spirit and activity. King Gillette, the razor man, began constructing a large home (later sold to Gloria Swanson) on Crescent Drive near Sunset. Others were also rising. A new street, Gwendolyn Drive (now Rexford) had been opened and a house was underway, to be occupied by a former Congressman from Kansas named W.A. Reeder.

The need for larger school facilities soon became apparent. Efforts to have Los Angeles County enlarge the Coldwater School failed. That, and a fear of a potential water shortage, prompted public sentiment for incorporation.

A petition was circulated. Approval called for 500 signatures, an impossible total for Beverly Hills to round up within its limits. It's said that the additional signatures were found just over the eastern border in Sherman. There, a group of itinerant workers were persuaded to live (temporarily, at least) at Lewis

North Cañon Drive, ca 1918.

North from Park Way (one block above Santa Monica Boulevard), ca 1918. Beverly Drive cuts upward through center of photo. Rodeo Drive at left, surrounded by tilled bean fields, has utility poles running along the length of the center strip.

Between the years 1912 and 1916, baseball games were played nearly every Saturday afternoon in the large circular space where Beverly, Cañon and Crescent Drives converge near the Beverly Hills Hotel. The city's team was called the "Bean-Eaters."

45

Station, a small "company" housing settlement for farmhands and city workers adjacent to the south side of the Pacific Electric tracks. Incorporation was granted on January 2, 1914. Twenty-one days later an election was held to name a governing Board of Trustees.

Within three months, the first of a series of quarrels with Los Angeles began. On April 25, the big neighbor began laying a pipeline across Coldwater Canyon on a right-of-way purchased from the Rodeo Land and Water Company. Clearly, the City of Beverly Hills had a case; the company had no jurisdiction over governing matters. A legal battle followed, ending in the courtroom. The decision, handed down in Superior Court, ultimately favored Los Angeles (the welfare of half a million people should have precedence over two or three hundred, it was argued)—but the Board of Trustees had, for the moment, established postion with the Rodeo Land and Water Company.

Looking east down Santa Monica Boulevard   ca 1918

The Burton Green estate on Lexington Road (below) was completed in 1914, the year Beverly Hills was incorporated. On the grounds was one of the first swimming pools in the city. Right, the Green home today with a totally new look for new owner Eugene V. Klein, President and Board Chairman of National General Corporation as well as owner of the San Diego Chargers.

The next few years were marked by steady progress. The Burton Green and Max Whittier estates were among the showplaces. A grammar school was under construction. Streets had been resurfaced and street lights installed. Hordes of Los Angelenos drove out to picnic or pick beans that were left in the surrounding fields after threshing. A "public transportation" system was inaugurated: a ramshackle Ford that putt-putted its way between the Pacific Electric Station and the hotel—shortly to be replaced by a one-car trolley system after being overturned in a collision with a Great Dane. Without a general store, shopping was

Oilman Kirk B. Johnson's stately hillside home atop Alpine Drive was one of the earliest in Beverly Hills, built around 1912.

Two of the most imposing early estates belonged to Roland P. Bishop (top) and Max Whittier. The Bishop mansion, set on a knoll behind the Beverly Hills Hotel, later became the residence of banker Irving Hellman. Whittier, oilman and one of the city's original developers, selected a site along Sunset Boulevard and was the first to bring the Italian Renaissance style of architecture to Beverly Hills. Opposite page: the Whittier mansion as it appears today.

Beverly Hills Grammar School on Rexford Drive (left), built in 1914, was renamed Hawthorne Grammar School in 1925. Above, the Hawthorne crest.

done in Los Angeles. But neighboring merchants refused to make individual deliveries to the scattered homes, so purchases (including milk, groceries and newspapers) were left at the P.E. Depot to be distributed by local good samaritans. This practice continued until the late teens when a single business building went up.

This was also a time of expansion. The voters had accepted a petition to annex an unincorporated portion of the old rancho, lying on the southeast boundary.

While the population growth remained relatively still, the boundaries were moving. To some, the progress within this beautiful new city, one unlike any other, had been a disappointment. Others seemed to be simply waiting it out. Little did anyone know that an incredible boom was just around the corner.

The new Hawthorne School building on the original Rexford site was constructed in 1929; additional facilities were completed in 1966, 1967 and 1970.

THE TWENTIES

The dawdling development of the first few years may have been cause for concern, but not for long. The new decade was full of surprises. It was almost as if the city had been biding its time, waiting to hitch its wagon to a star—literally.

Between 1920 and 1925, the population climbed from less than 700 people to 7,500. By 1926, it was 12,000. Business lots priced at $800 were going for $70,000 six years later. Beverly Hills became a gathering place: 35,000 Shriners assembled for a rodeo; horse, dog and flower shows became a tradition; the first "Round the World" flyers from Santa Monica were royally entertained; the National Editorial Association, and others, held conventions.

With the influx of people, the city's needs increased. Residents clamored for schools, churches, and the cry, "We want another park," was heard. Streets were paved, widened, extended and lighted. "Electrical semaphore signals" were installed, 34-hour airmail service to New York was inaugurated, new areas of the city were opened up. The city welcomed another hotel, a movie house, "talking" pictures and a newspaper. "Trade at Home Week" set out to prove for the first time that Beverly Hills had the finest shops and stores on the West Coast. Times were frantic. Madcap.

Only a local event of international importance seemed to bring everyone down to earth—for a moment, at least. A leading resident, Rudolph Valentino, had died.

Until the early 20s, before the boom really began, Beverly Drive was a peaceful, little-used byway.

54

START YOUR ENGINES

Road racing in Southern California had been a top sport for years. Starting in 1909, the "triangle" in Santa Monica (between the beach city and the Soldiers' Home at Sawtelle) was a natural racing course for young enthusiasts, as was the Speedway in Ocean Park and Venice. When public roads became an unsafe place to hold the events, and collecting spectators' fees became impossible, a syndicate headed by Peck and Caufield constructed a giant wood oval on a portion of their recently acquired land. Located just west of Beverly Drive and south of Wilshire Boulevard, their Speedway helped make the Southland Beverly Hills

conscious. Here, thousands of spectators could sit in comfort and watch the finest drivers of the day, including Ralph de Palma and his nephew Peter de Paolo, juggle with records and each other's lives. Engineers built speed into the Beverly Hills course. It measured one and one-quarter miles around and its spectacular turns were pitched at a "fearful angle" of 43 degrees so that a driver had to maintain acceleration to stay on them.

In its day the Speedway rivaled the Indianapolis 500; many of the same drivers and automobiles played the

The greatest names in motor racing appeared at the Beverly Hills Speedway in the early 20s, attracting crowds that jammed the grandstand and bleachers. The row of eucalyptus trees, cutting across center of photo, was a barrier against the winds that roared down from the canyons. Note scattered oil wells in lower left corner, reminders of a small strike in 1908.

Beverly Hills and its Speedway, 1923. Preuss Road (now Robertson Boulevard) cuts across bottom of photo; Pico Boulevard is at left. Olympic Boulevard had not yet been developed. Wilshire can be seen dotted with small trees, just above the windbreak of eucalyptus trees. The Speedway was demolished after the Washington Day race in 1924. By late that year, only the scars of the giant oval remained.

59

"circuit." While Indianapolis had its Memorial Day attraction, Beverly Hills had its Turkey Day race each Thanksgiving, as well as its Washington's Birthday event. In between, motorcycle races were held.

The first 200-lap Turkey Day race, won by Jimmy Murphy, took place in 1920. The last, and reportedly the best, was held three years later when the first five finishers shattered the world's record for distance.

In 1924, the Speedway was dismantled and the land was purchased by Walter G. McCarty for development. The famed oval was short-lived but the noise it generated for the city lingered long after the last lap.

The Speedway was demolished after the Washington Day race in 1924. By late that year, only the scars of the giant oval remained as the marking of a new development became noticeable. Beverly Drive (widest street cutting through center of photo) appears to have been recently extended southward while the future Olympic Boulevard is being charted.

*Gateway to Pickfair, one of the most
seen sights in Beverly Hills. Will Rogers
once remarked, "My most important
duty as Mayor is directing folks to
Mary Pickford's home."*

PICKFAIR

As the movies and their stars gained in popularity and
affluence, a new mark of distinction slowly emerged.
In 1909, Douglas Fairbanks began construction on his
Grayhall estate just west of the Beverly Hills boundary.
Ten years later, he crossed the line to build a spacious
home high in the foothills which he occupied, after his
marriage in March, 1920, with his young bride, Mary
Pickford.

The reigning King and Queen of Hollywood had
moved to Beverly Hills. The world took note and soon
Pickfair, as the press had named it, was making
headlines for its lavish parties and innumerable charitable affairs.

*Pickfair from the air, 1924. Zero, Mary and
Doug's beloved airedale, had the run of the estate
while their two cows were kept at the foot of the
hill.*

The stately living room at Pickfair, 1920s. Over the years, it has been the scene of innumerable gatherings attended by royalty and the greats from every field. In meetings at Pickfair, film notables conceived the idea of the Academy of Motion Picture Arts and Sciences, as well as United Artists studio.

Today, cherubs welcome visitors at the main entrance to Pickfair, home of Mary Pickford and Charles "Buddy" Rogers.

The heart of the Beverly Hills business district, 1922. Beverly Drive, north from Brighton Way.

Sketch of "new" Pacific Electric Station, "to be constructed on the west side of Cañon Drive," late 1931. The architecture was selected to tie in with the then-rising civic center.

At the turn of the century, Beverly Hills was little more than a whistle-stop called Morocco Junction, a far from glamorous transfer point for Santa Monica-bound passengers. For their convenience, the Pacific Electric provided a depot which boasted a makeshift stand where peanuts, newspapers and refreshments were available, and an outhouse. By 1911, with the running time from downtown Los Angeles only 32 minutes, train traffic had increased—but not many people cared. They were too anxious to keep going. When the 20s arrived (right), it was a different story. Beverly Hills was on the map and the little stopping point had become a center of local activity.

Will Rogers

Mary Pickford

Fred Niblo

Douglas Fairbanks

Harold Lloyd

Conrad Nagle

Rudolph Valentino

Tom Mix

ANNEXATION
OR STAGNATION

As the young city's numbers continued to grow, water became a major concern. The Beverly Hills Utility Company, a subsidiary of the Rodeo Land and Water Company, announced that its few shallow wells in Coldwater Canyon could no longer provide enough water to meet the needs of the population. It was anxious to turn the problem over to the City of Los Angeles and suggested annexation. The town was immediately divided. One side claimed that "the growing tentacles of Los Angeles sought to include Beverly Hills within its jurisdiction to derive all the benefits of a rich residential district—for the small return of water privileges." Others touted, "Annexation or stagnation!" The city sued to inforce its contract while the Company, through petitioning, was able to force a special election. Campaigning for both sides was fierce.

Election morning, April 24, was bedlam. Those favoring annexation had made the rounds, delivering to the doorstep of every residence a milk bottle containing foul smelling sulphur water. Attached to each bottle was a warning: "This is a sample of the water which the Trustees of the City of Beverly Hills propose for our city. Drink sparingly as it has laxative qualities!"

The "anti" forces barely had time to counter—but they did in stunning fashion. Led by eight of the movies' brightest stars, all residents, they made their way through the streets chanting a "No" vote on annexation, and accepting pledges in exchange for autographed glossy photos.

That evening, as the votes were being counted, knots of residents gathered on street corners and in front of the old City Hall on Canon Drive. Beverly Hills' fate was in limbo. But not for long. The city's independence, and individuality, had been saved by a count of 507 to 337. The victory news set the stage for what probably was the city's first street dance. Fire sirens screamed as a brass band quickly formed to serenade the ecstatic crowd with "There'll Be A Hot Time In The Old Town Tonight."

The defeat of annexation marked the end of the Utility Company. A few months later, it sold out for $250,000, paving the way for development of Beverly Hills' own well and water system.

Corinne Griffith led the crusade to memorialize the stars who helped save Beverly Hills' independence in 1923. Their monument, at the intersection of Beverly Drive and Olympic Boulevard was dedicated in 1959

When the Beverly Hills Hotel opened, it became obvious that transportation had to be provided for the convenience of visitors and guests, particularly those arriving at the depot. Eventually, the Pacific Electric installed tracks down the center strip of Rodeo Drive from Santa Monica Boulevard to Sunset and east past the hotel, and shuttle service began.

The deed from the Rodeo Land & Water Company to the Pacific Electric contained a reversionary clause to the effect that should its use for railroad purposes be discontinued, the strip would revert to the Rodeo

Company. By 1923, the P.E. "dinky" to and from the hotel had been discontinued for some time.

The right-of-way along Sunset and Rodeo was an open clay strip and an eyesore, just waiting to be put to good use. The answer came when Stanley Anderson, husband of the Beverly Hills Hotel's Margaret Anderson, and banker Irving Hellman organized and incorporated the Bridle Path Association.

During a dinner meeting at the hotel, enough money was raised to extend the path to Doheny Drive, surface it with decomposed granite, and plant a hedge of flowering shrubs on both sides of its entire length. Many prominent attendees contributed substantially, among them Milton Goetz, Ben Myers, Silsby Spalding, Burton Green, Max Whittier and Will Rogers.

The bridle trail down Sunset and Rodeo, which fostered considerable interest in horseback riding in the community, became a must-see sight for visitors. To the west, it joined other trails that wandered to the ocean; to the north, it was extended along Benedict Canyon Drive where it connected with many trails and paths in the mountains. With the heavy increase in car traffic after World War II, "Ye Bridle Path" was removed and landscaped.

Looking west down Sunset Boulevard through "Ye Bridle Path" arch at the Canon Drive crossing, 1931. Inset, equestrian group along Rodeo Drive trail, 1925.

Traffic jam at the intersection of Wilshire and Santa Monica Boulevards—part of a staged demonstration to obtain traffic signals for the narrow, much-traveled crossing, 1924.

In 1923, the then Roman Catholic Bishop of Los Angeles, Most Reverend John Joseph Cantwell, established a parish in Beverly Hills and gave it its present name. The following year, the mission-style Church of the Good Shepherd, with its landmark twin golden domes, was erected at the corner of Santa Monica Boulevard and Bedford Drive; dedication was held on February 1, 1925. During the construction period, Sunday Mass was offered to the Catholic families in the community in the Terrace Room of the Beverly Hills Hotel. Major modernization of the church, interior and exterior, was completed in 1959.

Opposite page, exterior of the original Church of the Good Shepherd, erected in 1924; right, after reconstruction in 1959.

Interior of the church, post 1959.

*Above, carved mission-style doors
at the main entry to the church.
Right, the Good Shepherd
protecting his flock.*

South from Tower Road, above the Beverly Hills Hotel, 1924. Note the terraced agricultural land. Many realtors were touting acreage already planted with avocado and citrus trees, saying "the crops will more than pay the taxes."

Reverse view, looking north past growing Little Santa Monica Boulevard business area, 1924. The ratio of homes versus vacant land appears to be equalizing.

RESIDENCES

Falcon Lair, home of Rudolph Valentino.

The immense popularity of Pickfair, with its beautiful setting and magnificent panoramic views, soon prompted other notables to leave the confines and traffic of bustling Los Angeles and Hollywood. The stars were moving in—the invasion was on!

Gloria Swanson, Pola Negri, Tom Mix and Richard Barthelmess, all top movie names, had come to Beverly Hills. But so did others equally famous: Charlie Chaplin, Rudolph Valentino, Wallace Beery, Buster Keaton, The Talmadges (Constance and Norma), Jeannette MacDonald, Will Rogers, Conrad Nagle, Marion Davies, and more.

The list was not limited to movie stars. With far less ballyhoo, others of prominence flocked in. Fannie Hearst, P.G. Wodehouse, Charles MacArthur, Fred Niblo, Dorothy Parker, Louis B. Mayer, Thomas Ince, Louella Parsons, Sam Goldwyn, Carl Laemmle, Dashiel Hammett, Jasha Heifetz, S.N. Behrman, Arturo Rubinstein all made Beverly Hills their home. Sightseers and reporters were having a field day. Suddenly, Beverly Hills itself had turned celebrity.

Top, the residence of Tom Mix; right, the Will Rogers estate.

Above (clockwise): The homes of Conrad Veidt; Theda Bara; Norma Talmadge; Charles Chaplin. Opposite page, John Barrymore.

The "storybook" home of Hans Kraley (one of the giants of silent films in Germany), a Beverly Hills legend for years. While it is often thought to have been built originally as a movie set, it was actually the replica of a style Kraley recalled from his days in Normandy and tried to duplicate after his arrival in this country following World War I. An Academy Award-winning screenwriter, he worked with Ernst Lubitch, another Beverly Hills resident, on many early films. Above, the home as it appears today.

Right, the residence of Ruth Chatterton and Ralph Forbes. Below, the home of Ben Turpin.

The home of Corinne Griffith.

"Dias Dorados," the home of Thomas H. Ince. He was the first of the studio heads to move to Beverly Hills and introduced a lifestyle that came to be known as "Hollywood."

Homes of the stars were of great
interest to visitors even in the 20s.
Tanner Motor Tours was the first to
organize sightseeing excursions of the
famous Beverly Hills homes. Right,
with megaphone in hand, a guide
directs attention toward the residence
of Gloria Swanson.

In October, 1916, a group of forty women gathered to form an organization through which charitable work might be carried on; at the same time, to offer an opportunity for newcomers to the community to make acquaintances and be of service. From this initial meeting evolved the Beverly Hills Women's Club. Aside from the city itself, it is the second oldest incorporation in the area.

In 1924, the Club joined the General Federation of Women's Clubs. The following year, an imposing club house opened on the southwest corner of Benedict Canyon and Chevy Chase Drives, since designated an historic site (page 14). The search to find a suitable location was not without struggle and disappointment, however. Several sites had been selected previously, one at the corner of Sunset Boulevard and Crescent Drive was thought particularly favorable. "Building restrictions imposed such strict limitations," noted one club official, "that members despaired of ever procuring a suitable site."

Over the years, the Beverly Hills Women's Club has supported and contributed to a varied number of philanthropic and civic enterprises, including the Red Cross, Scholarship Loan Fund, Friends of the Library and many others.

Left, the Club House on Chevy Chase Drive shortly after completion in 1925. Below, Mrs. Jay B. Millard (with shovel) is joined by members of Beverly Hills Women's Club at ground-breaking ceremony for new headquarters, ca 1924.

In 1917, during the battle at Chateau Thierry in France, a boy and a statue became casualties of World War I. The boy was the son of W.D. Longyear, pioneer Beverly Hills resident. The statue, which stood over a deep vaulted cellar built by American troops, was "Hunter and Hounds," the work of Henri Alfred Marie Jacquemart. To memorialize his son, Mr. Longyear obtained special permission from the French government to bring the shell-scarred statue to the United States. On November 11, 1925, it was unveiled and dedicated on the lawn of the Longyear estate (left center in photo, opposite page). Memorial ceremonies were held each Armistice Day for many years with local officials and members of the Beverly Hills American Legion Post participating. "Hunter and Hounds" was since donated to the city and is now in the park along Santa Monica Boulevard, not far from the Longyear family home off Beverly Drive.

The bond issues of 1923 and 1924, which provided monies for additions to the original Hawthorne School, also paved the way for the construction of a second elementary school in the city. In 1925, on twenty-eight lots in the 200 block of South Elm Drive, Beverly Vista School was dedicated. An impressive brick structure, it immediately filled the need for more classrooms in the fastest growing section of the community. Beverly Hills was expanding at a greater pace than anyone had imagined, however. Within a year, Beverly Vista was overcrowded. Another bond issue was passed to pay for additional facilities, at the same time, paving the way for a third grammar school on the west side of town.

Starting in 1925, Beverly Hills became noted for its series of annual Horse Shows, many of which were sponsored by the Beverly Hills Women's Club, the Chamber of Commerce and the Bridle Path Association. The competition pitted local entries against blue bloods from across the country; one train load from Denver was tabbed the "Million Dollar Special" because of the value of the show horses it carried.

The first Horse Show was held on Saturday, January 10 in a huge arena constructed just off the bridle path at Sunset Boulevard and Roxbury Drive. Subsequent shows were held at the Los Angeles Riding Club on Preuss Road (now Robertson Boulevard) and Beverly Boulevard.

At the "First Annual Open Air Beverly Hills Equestrian Pageant," its official name, the box holders included Miss Cecilia Hoyt de Mille, Nacio Herb Brown, Hobart Bosworth, Walter G. McCarty, Douglas Fairbanks and Miss Ruth Roland.

One of the highlights of the 1925 Beverly Hills Horse Show was the festive parade along the Sunset Boulevard bridle path.

(Above) The Polo Club entry takes its turn in the ring, 1925. (Below) Will Rogers sat in Box 75 at the first annual "Pageant."

99

Berkeley Hall School, a private institution, was established in 1911 in a small English cottage on Western Avenue in Los Angeles. In the mid-'20s, it was relocated to its present address on North Swall Drive in Beverly Hills. With the move, the school retained the architectural flavor of its beginnings, the new classrooms being housed in six units of English-style structures clustered about a central green. In 1932, feeling that Berkeley Hall School had grown beyond the bounds of personal ownership, the founders selected a Board of Trustees to insure its future.

In 1925, the residents voted to join Los Angeles, Santa Monica and Venice in helping to purchase a new 385-acre site for the southern campus of the University of California, which had outgrown its facilities in mid-town Los Angeles. The city's share was $100,000, to be carried through a bond issue. So strongly did the people want the university in nearby Westwood, then little more than a rolling bean field, that campaigning became a popular cause. Coeds roamed the business district, distributing posters and leaflets to shoppers, urging them to vote "yes." Because of its participation in the successful venture and its pride in the new campus, Beverly Hills billed itself for a time as "The University City."

The dedication of Kerckhoff Hall on the UCLA campus, January 20, 1931. The building was a gift to the university by Mrs. William G. Kerckhoff (third from left), whose husband was one of the original group that founded Beverly Hills.

The Beverly Hills American Legion Post 253 was established in 1926 under the command of Charles Woods; the Auxiliary (women's) group in the 30s to assist in its activities. Legion Hall, the community club house on Robertson Boulevard, was dedicated in 1937, due largely to the leadership and financial assistance of then Commander Sam Hahn. A noted attorney, Hahn was a guiding force both in the Post and in civic affairs.

Beverly Vista Presbyterian Church.

The Beverly Hills Community Church was organized in August, 1921, with twenty-two charter members. A charter site, at Rodeo Drive and Santa Monica Boulevard, was provided by the Rodeo Land & Water Company. Four years later, the church itself was under construction and in February, 1926, dedication ceremonies were held. By 1950, the church had outgrown the original building and the north wing with its chapel, lounging and convocation hall, was added.

The Beverly Vista Church, organized in February, 1927, as a missionary extension program of the United Presbyterian Church in North America, held its first meeting in the music room of the then new Beverly Vista School. Construction on the church began in 1928; additions were completed in 1940 and 1948.

In September, 1972, the two congregations voted to join forces, becoming the Beverly Hills Presbyterian Church.

*Beverly Hills Presbyterian Church
(formerly Beverly Hills Community
Church).*

The church tower at Rodeo Drive and
Santa Monica Boulevard has been a
landmark for fifty years.

By 1950, the church had outgrown the original building and the north wing was added.

In 1922, a small group of people gathered in the game room of the Beverly Hills Hotel for Episcopal worship. Four years later, $26,000 had been raised to buy the land to build the original chapel at Camden Drive and Santa Monica Boulevard. By 1935, All Saints' had become a parish and, with it, continued growth and development. It soon became apparent that a larger church building and parish house facilities would be needed. The buildings were completed and dedicated in 1951 and the original church was preserved for use as the chapel.

All Saints' Episcopal Church.

The church addition, dedicated in 1951, echoes the Spanish Colonial design of the original chapel.

Leafy silhouettes play on the flagstone surface of the entry courtyard.

The delicate stained glass windows were designed and installed by the late Charles Connick of Boston and Whitefriars of London.

To Pick His
ORANGES
We Love Our
DOUG..
But Oh You
Beverly Hills
WELCOMES
MAYOR WILL
HOME
To
THAW OUT
MAYOR
Y HILLS
COMES—

WELCOME HOME!

Will Rogers was a star on Broadway and in motion pictures. He was a syndicated writer with world-wide popularity (his dateline "Beverly Hills" was worth millions in publicity), and one of the greatest humorists of all time. In 1926, his "Letters of a Self-Made Diplomat to His President" had been published in the *Saturday Evening Post* to great acclaim. He was returning home from a triumphant tour of Europe when, as the story goes, someone casually remarked that Beverly Hills had no Mayor (an honorary title as, at that time, the city's presiding officer was President of the Board of Trustees). The simple statement triggered his adoring neighbors to action. Will was met at the train station in downtown Los Angeles by a long line of Rolls Royces and other fancy cars and escorted to the grounds of the Beverly Hills Hotel where, despite a light rain, the stage was set. Townsfolk waving placards and banners crowded around a plat-form bedecked with bunting and chanted for "Mayor Will." Douglas Fairbanks clasped his hand and said, "We have gathered here to welcome Will Rogers home." Motion picture stars presented him with the key to the city done in flowers. Before Rogers fully realized what was happening, he had been "elected." Few people in the crowd felt that the activities would create more than local interest—but the Associated Press picked up the story and it became news from coast to coast.

The following year, the California Legislature amended the Municipal Corporations Act so that the Trustees were known as Councilmen and the President as Mayor. That action let Will Rogers off the hook. When he received word, he is said to have remarked that if he had known Beverly Hills was only a city of the sixth class he never would have had anything to do with it.

El Rodeo, overlooking Los Angeles Country Club on the western edge of the city, was another indication of the phenomenal surge of the 20s. With Hawthorne and Beverly Vista Schools overflowing, additional space for the increasing number of children became necessary. A site on Whittier Drive and the then lightly traveled Wilshire Boulevard was selected and named in honor of the original land grant, El Rodeo de las Aguas. Had this valuable land not been claimed for the school, a portion of it would have undoubtedly been used, within the next few years, as an extension of the park system.

Upon completion, El Rodeo won awards for its striking architectural design. It has long been noted as one of the most beautiful schools in the country. Right, El Rodeo, ca 1930; below, as it looks today.

Beverly Hills High School taken from the back lot of the Fox Studios (now the site of Century City).

Until 1927, students of secondary school age in Beverly Hills were forced to attend various high schools outside the city limits. For years, demands for a local high school were common but unconvincing with a hesitant Los Angeles School Board. But pressures from the Women's Club, civic organizations and service clubs finally brought results and the Board agreed to build and maintain a high school in Beverly Hills. In the fall of 1927, a structure of French Normandy design was opened on a plot of ground that cost $166,000.

The battle was only half won. Two factors soon pointed to the advisability of the city taking over the high school: the importance of a unified school system and the cost to Beverly Hills taxpayers of maintaining the school. (It would cost less annually for the city to run it than the payments to the Los Angeles system.) In the fall of 1930, the fight to take over the high school began. Only after the local citizens had secured passage of a state law, one enabling a city to take over a system under the existing circumstances, did the campaign prove successfull. On July 1, 1935, the local board took over the jurisdiction of the high school. The following year, the Beverly Hills elementary and high school districts became the first unified district in the state.

Right, the attendance office; below, the original faculty that opened the high school in 1927. Included in the group is its first principal, Ralph D. Wadsworth (fourth from left).

The Goodyear blimp created a stir among students and faculty when it landed on campus for a surprise visit, May 10, 1930.

For three consecutive years, starting January 1, 1927, Beverly Hills' entries in the annual Tournament of Roses in Pasadena walked off with top honors—First Prize and Sweepstakes. And to complete the coup, the flower girls won First in their class, as well. The awards brought tremendous publicity to the city, as evidenced by this item from a 1928 pamphlet: "Twenty-five million people heard and marveled at the radio description of the float. Another 25 million people saw it on the motion-picture screen. Thousands of pictures were printed in papers and magazines, with glorifying captions appended. Other thousands of articles were written about the entry. In 1928, this publicity grew even greater, owing to the fact that the triumph of 1927 was repeated. This was the first time in the Rose Tournament's history that both prizes were won in successive years by any city!"

And history had yet to record still another triumph the following year.

122

By 1927, the population growth was such that it was obvious new water sources would have to be developed. It was decided to purchase, if possible, the Union-Hollywood Water Company, then owning some producing wells, extensive underground water rights and a distribution system serving all of Sherman (now West Hollywood). Considerable bickering highlighted the lengthy negotiations but, ultimately, the city purchased the water company for $400,000. A bond issue was passed and a plant for softening and filtering the new water was constructed at LaCienega and Olympic Boulevards.

THE GIFT

In the late 1800s, Edward L. Doheny, a poor young man of Irish descent headed west from Wisconsin to make his fortune. He did just that in oil, many times over.

Acquiring a ranch of 410 acres, he decided to use a portion of the property to build a gift for Edward Jr., his only son. Greystone, a mammoth, modern-day castle, was that gift.

Construction on the Greystone Mansion began in 1925 and was completed in 1928 at a cost of over $4 million (estimates today hover around $50 million). Situated high on a knoll overlooking the entire Los Angeles basin and Santa Monica Bay, the mansion and its surrounding grounds, executed in grand European style, became a triumph of architectural and landscaping art.

Marble and tile of varying shades, rare woods, furnishings, even the decorative slate adorning the roof, were imported. Workmanship was the finest. After installation of the banisters, balustrades and rafters, Doheny imported artisans to carve them in place. The work took about two years.

Within its 46,000 square feet and 55 rooms, Greystone included a grand dining room with its own balcony from which an orchestra played; a ladies' powder room the size of a one-bedroom apartment; a chapel; a bowling alley; and a separate kitchen for the children's wing (there were five in the family). Additionally, three floors were devoted to the servants' quarters for a live-in staff of 36.

The Doheny family occupied the estate until 1955. When the land was then sold, subdivision of the priceless property seemed inevitable. In 1964, however, the City of Beverly Hills acquired the estate. Even then, destruction of the mansion itself appeared likely. Fortunately, the half-million dollars needed to demolish the building, constructed throughout of steel-reinforced concrete (the walls are three feet thick), discouraged the plan and it was preserved as a passive retreat for the community's urban population. Greystone was formally dedicated as a park in September, 1971. The grounds include 16 acres of formal gardens, wooded acres, orchards, pools, lawns and picturesque walkways.

The Greystone Mansion is presently leased to the American Film Institute as a center for advanced film studies.

The arrival court, Greystone Mansion.

Above, aerial shot of the newly completed mansion and gardens, 1929. Right, a wooded drive, leuding to the mansion.

The grounds of Greystone are landscaped in the grand European style with formal terraced gardens and walkways.

The original swimming pool (right) has since been partially filled in to become a reflection pool. During garden parties, orchestras played from the roof of the pool house.

Each of the mansion's chimneys is handmade in a different design.

Right, the Doheny children's "dollhouse," a 7-room English-style cottage. It was eventually turned into a guest house. Below, the original entry with adjoining gatekeeper's lodge.

When Greystone was acquired by the city in 1964, a much needed reservoir, capable of holding 19 million gallons of water, was constructed beneath the upper parking lot. The reservoir now supplies Beverly Hills with 45% of its water. Here shown prior to filling.

The mansion roof is covered with 2″ to 3″ thick Welsh slate; the rain gutters and drainage pipes are of solid lead. Noted architects and engineers have called Greystone a pyramid of modern times.

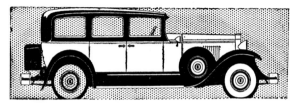

A Call For
1926, '27 and '28
HUPMOBILES

We urgently request the owners of 1926, 1927 and 1928 Hupmobiles to trade in their cars now on new Hupmobile Century Sixes or Eights. This request is made because of the tremendous demand for these popular Hupmobile models — a demand our used car supply does not permit us to fulfill.

Due to this demand and Hupmobile's exceptionally high resale value we are now in a position to offer a very attractive allowance on Hupmobiles sold during the past three years.

If you are the owner of a 1926, 1927 or 1928 Hupmobile — either six or eight — it will be to your advantage — and ours, too — if you trade it in now. When the demand exceeds the supply the market value is necessarily higher.

Important Notice

Hupmobile's new program of expansion has reduced all prices . . . some up to $260.00.

SUMMERIL *and* BRADLEY
Hupmobile Dealers

441 N. Camden Dr.   OXford 7034

ADVERTISING

South on Beverly Drive from Brighton Way, 1928.

GREENACRES

In 1928, at the peak of his career, Harold Lloyd began construction on one of the true, man-made wonders, Greenacres. Here, on the slopes of Benedict Canyon, rose the ideal movie star's hideaway, a palatially private "Shangri-La."

Designed on a grand scale, the $2 million, two-story mansion was a showplace from the beginning. Its 44 rooms included a 60-foot long main entry hall, an enormous gallery with timbered ceiling and great arched doorways, a mammoth drawing room (which doubled as a theater) dominated by a massive hand-hewn fireplace wall, and a solarium. (The garden room was famous for the ornate Christmas tree, laden with over 5,000 heirloom ornaments, which remained year-round for all to enjoy. The last tree that Mr. Lloyd helped decorate stood for 10 years.) All of the main rooms, oversized and ornate, were distinguished by either tile or parquet floors, paneled walls or hand-painted ceilings in the Italian Renaissance style.

The house, however spectacular, was overshadowed by its surroundings. Gardens of every nature were everywhere. The entry drive, winding through nearly a mile of heavily wooded forests, passed streams and cascading waterfalls. A small lake, stocked with fish, boasted a boat house and an authentic Dutch style windmill. Huge, bubbling fountains were focal points on every level, as well as in the swimming pool. Pavilions, pergolas and pools added dramatic elegance. The children's garden, complete with a miniature storybook farmhouse and adjoining stable, were furnished in every detail down to tiny bales of hay.

Greenacres was the epitome of a star's home. It is only fitting that for several years after Harold Lloyd's death in 1971, the estate became a favorite location site for motion pictures and television.

Harold Lloyd relaxes in the garden of his Italian Renaissance-style estate, Greenacres.

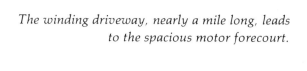

The winding driveway, nearly a mile long, leads to the spacious motor forecourt.

A man-made stream, a brownstone bridge and a miniature lake, complete with boathouse and windmill, are among the sights visitors first see at Greenacres.

140

The expansive carpet of lawn and surrounding dense foliage gave Greenacres its name. The columnar structure (center of photo and insert) is a chimney for an underground room.

The long garden, flanked by beds of roses and tall trees, contains a decorative fountain at one end and an imposing tea pavilion at the other.

145

The Olympic-size swimming pool, tiled green and white, with its bubbly fountain at the wading end. A curving arbor, covered with grape and wisteria vines, offers protection from the sun.

Guests relax around the pool house and pool during an informal party, 1940s.

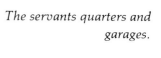

The children's garden with its small-scale "Hansel and Gretel" farmhouse and stable. It was furnished in every detail, down to miniature bales of hay (including electricity and running water).

148

The reflection pool, surrounded by stately planted urns, contains splashing fountains and flowing lilies. At the far end, a concrete pergola in the Mediterranean style, seems to rise from the water.

The waterfall garden at Greenacres. Water from a huge stone basin trickles downward through a series of smaller basins that form the centerpiece of a long cobblestone corridor. At its end, another fountain, centered in a circular landing paved in a mosaic of colored stones.

Massive, opulent showplaces appeared on the northern and western edges of Beverly Hills throughout the 20s. It was an incredible architectural era that was soon to end forevermore.

Right, the sprawling estate of Mr. Carrie Guggenheim, member of the prominent steel family. Below, the English-style mansion of industrialist George Lewis. Opposite page, the palatial Sunset Boulevard "town house" estate of Francis V. Betiller.

The year 1928 was brought in with more razzle-dazzle than usual. The occasion was the opening of what was termed "the last word in an apartment hotel." Nothing less than a gigantic New Year's Eve party would do to christen the magnificent, new Beverly Wilshire Hotel. "Over $3 million have been spent," boasted the papers, "in making this the most elaborately built and furnished hotel in the United States." The original Beverly Wilshire towered nine stories high and contained 350 hotel rooms and apartments, two basements, six public rooms and eight shops.

With the opening of the hotel, one columnist stated,

"The Beverly Wilshire stands, and ever will stand, as a monument to the loyalty and love that Walter Mc-Carty, the builder, bears for his home city."

Walter G. McCarty was instrumental in developing at least 50 subdivisions in the Los Angeles-Beverly Hills area. With the demise of the Beverly Hills Speedway, he and his associates purchased the track site and more for $2 million, dividing the land into business and residential lots. A large portion of the property along Wilshire Boulevard was reserved as a hotel site. The Beverly Wilshire became an immediate landmark and was, for years, the city's tallest structure.

154

The elegant entrance to the Beverly Wilshire Hotel, 1928.

The Beverly Hills Nursery, at "the point" created by the crossing of Wilshire and Santa Monica Boulevards, was one of the largest retail nurseries in Southern California. Dating back to the earliest days of the city, it was created to supply the city's landscaping needs. Originally located off Sunset Boulevard on the northeastern side of town, it moved to "the point" in the mid-20s and occupied that spot until the 40s. The land is now the site of the Beverly Hilton Hotel and Robinson's Beverly.

Boy Scouts take part in dedication of new Chamber of Commerce headquarters, at northeast corner of Beverly Drive and Little Santa Monica Boulevard, in January, 1929. Organized in 1923, the Chamber has staunchly followed its creed " . . . to promote the economic, commercial, industrial, civic and social welfare of the people of the City of Beverly Hills and vicinity . . ." and has become one of the most involved and influencial forces in the community. During its first 25 years, the Chamber occupied nine different locations. In 1948, it acquired property on South Beverly Drive; formal opening of its new building was held on April 18, 1949.

Almost from the beginning, the Chamber of Commerce Annual Banquet was one of the most sought-after "tickets" in town, being frequently compared to the famous Gridiron Dinner in Washington. Fred Niblo served for several years as Toastmaster while many noted residents contributed their talents when called upon. Appearing over the years have been such celebrities as Douglas Fairbanks, Mary Pickford, Tom Mix, Harold Lloyd, Jack Benny, Red Skelton, Jimmy Durante, Danny Thomas, Dinah Shore, Phil Harris, Dick Powell, Peggy Lee, Dorothy Lamour, Victor Borge and many more.

Toward the end of the 20s, the Chamber of Commerce produced what was advertised as "the biggest social or other public event of the season," the Beverly Hills Society Circus. On a ten-acre plot near the junction of Santa Monica and Wilshire Boulevards, a midway and giant tents were set up for the production which featured all the popular circus acts of the day: bareback riding, aerial ballet, hanging by teeth, horses and clowns, and others. Over 4,000 seats were available at prices ranging from $1 for general admission to $25 per box. The event was such a favorite it was broadcast over the radio.

159

HORACE MANN SCHOOL

·8701·

The opening of El Rodeo School on the west side of the city relieved the crowded classroom situation, but only temporarily. It was soon clear that still another elementary school was necessary. A site was selected in the southeastern section of the city, one that would give Beverly Hills the needed facilities to cover each of the prime population areas. In December, 1929, Horace Mann School was completed at a cost of $232,000. Beverly Hills now had four elementary schools: Hawthorne, Beverly Vista, El Rodeo and Horace Mann.

161

In only ten short years, Beverly Hills had turned from a "village" to a thriving city, one with "star status." The Great Depression had just hit the nation but the immediate news made little impression upon the illustrious residents. They were too busy making their own: Mary Pickford had bobbed her famous curls and Will Rogers was being touted for President by *Life* Magazine. Fox Studios, across the western edge of the city, had opened and was in full production. Articles were publicizing the city as "beautifully rural, conveniently urban," noting that "motorists may observe the traffic regulations and still reach the heart of Los Angeles within 25 minutes." About all the townsfolk had to fear was the demise of their quaint shopping area to the rush of newcomers. "We have defied the voracious commercial urge of the times," one civic official stated, trying to ease the concern, "and have firmly and definitely set the bounds of our business district. It is just large enough to serve the residents efficiently, and it will never be, *can* never be larger."

Looking west across Olympic Boulevard and Beverly Drive, late 1929. Note the macadam surfacing on Beverly Drive ends just prior to reaching Olympic. Large building in center of photo is the Beverly Wilshire Hotel.

THE THIRTIES

Despite the Depression, a census of that period showed a 52 percent gain—an indication of the fundamental strength of the still young city. Although an Unemployment Bureau was established, and streets and alleys were dotted with WPA workers on improvement projects, the city's increasing pride in itself was being tested and put to the task of creating an upswing in the economy. Across the city's eastern boundary in West Hollywood, a gimmick-game called "Prosperity Sam, the Movie Man" was created to lure money-hungry neighbors into the Marquis Theater. Not in Beverly Hills. Civic leaders that had grown with the boom years joined with energetic newcomers to work toward more lasting, positive ends. The business section, dubbed "The Triangle" because of its shape (bounded by Beverly Drive on the east and the crossing of Santa Monica and Wilshire Boulevards on the west), began the 30s with all three points competing against one another for local business. By the end of the decade, thanks to non-stop promotional activities, The Triangle was a combined force, now competing against Los Angeles for its trade. Beverly Hills was waging an upbeat campaign, playing on its image. Billboards were ordered off Wilshire Boulevard. Specialty shops were born. When Saks Fifth Avenue opened a store, ads blazed "New York comes to Beverly Hills." Suddenly, the city's shoppers were being recognized as "the most exacting," while the area itself was gaining a reputation as a "show window of the world." One reporter noted that "as center of the motion picture industry, Beverly Hills is replacing Paris and London in dictating the fashions." The Chamber of Commerce was having a field day. Their slogan: Beverly Hills—Center of the Next Million.

Looking west along Wilshire Boulevard, 1930.
Later that year, Bank of Italy (left center in
photo) became known as Bank of America.

By 1930, a growing number of new enterprises, and customers, were being attracted to the business district. Beverly Drive, looking north from Brighton Way.

For many years, the town of Altadena had been famous for its mile-long lane of brilliantly lighted trees at Christmas time. Beverly Hills had one tree, sponsored by the Community Church and called the Community Christmas Tree. When the church asked the city to take over sponsorship, Mary Pickford decided it was time to give Altadena a run for its money. She wanted to see not one tree but hundreds of lighted trees on the spacious lawns of her city and formed a committee to carry out her plan. Then she sent out personally signed letters to over 200 selected residents, those with beautiful evergreens, urging them to "light up." Not surprisingly, everyone complied with her request. Those who weren't asked hastily planted trees so they might participate the following year. The campaign was a tremendous success and attracted thousands of visitors each year to see what was soon called "Christmas Nights."

The lighted trees of (left) pioneer banker Irving Hellman and (below) director Ernst Lubitsch.

Beverly Hills' most famous Christmas tree, the Community Christmas tree, was a giant evergreen in the parkland along Santa Monica Boulevard. Each year, the lighting ceremony attracted huge crowds. The group on stage is the original "Beverly Hill Billys." Ca 1930.

Beverly Hills Catholic School on South Linden Drive opened in September, 1930. The Sisters of the Holy Cross, whose Mother House is located at Notre Dame, Indiana, staffed the school. Initially, there were eight grades; it wasn't until 1948 that kindergarten classes began. The Spanish architecture of the school was selected to harmonize with the Church of the Good Shepherd.

171

In the early 30s, all three corners of the business triangle were competing against each other for the local trade. Caillet Pharmacy, bounded by Wilshire and Little Santa Monica Boulevards, was on the western point. Armstrong-Schroder Cafe, one of Beverly Hills' all-time popular eating places, can be seen on the right.

BY POPULAR DEMAND

One night in 1925, Herbert K. Somborn was chatting with Abe Frank, Manager of Los Angeles' Ambassador Hotel, and Sid Grauman, of Chinese Theater fame, reflecting on the sorry state of the local restaurant scene. "You could open a restaurant in an alley and call it anything," he remarked, "and if the food and service were good the patrons would come flocking." Somborn hired a young friend, Robert H. Cobb, who had been raised in the business, and set out to prove his point. The original Brown Derby opened in Los Angeles in 1926, followed by the Hollywood location in 1929.

The patrons did flock; among them, a high number of celebrities. The Derbies soon became *the* place to eat and be seen, and it wasn't long before the people of Beverly Hills wanted one for their very own. In 1931, on the corner of Wilshire Boulevard and Rodeo Drive, the Beverly Hills Brown Derby opened. Immediately, it became one of the city's favorite gathering spots for the brightest names in society and motion pictures.

The Brown Derby, early 1930s.

The Derby's popular "King," Bob Cobb (left), trades hats with "King of the Cowboys," Tom Mix.

The Olde-English influence is seen in the original Brown Derby bar, the Derby House. Many celebrities would sit only at "their own" booths.

The Derby today. Except for the decor, it hasn't changed much over the years. It has long been known for its specialty items, such as Cobb Salad, created one night by accident. The famous charcoal drawings of Academy Award winners are by artist Nicholas Volpe.

The stars clamored for a Brown Derby in Beverly Hills and got one in 1931. Here, three of the all-time greats: Ruby Keeler, Eddie Cantor and Al Jolson. Ca 1938.

BEVERLY GARDENS

The master plan for Beverly Hills, as originally conceived, was carefully thought out and detailed in order to create the most spectacular residential development possible. Gently curving streets, extra-spacious homesites, generous setbacks for landscaping, and parks. Acres and acres of parks. Perhaps it was an overreaction to the stark stretches of bean fields, coupled with the swirling clouds of field dust, that prompted the developers to create an Eden. Whatever it was, they made a point to demand massive areas of plantings.

Despite their good intentions, only two parks existed in the main sections of Beverly Hills until the early 1930s: the picturesque triangle at the foot of the Beverly Hills Hotel, and the three-block parcel called Santa Monica Park that served to whet potential buyers' appetites nearly twenty years earlier. During the 20s, however, signs of progress along Santa Monica Boulevard were beginning to rattle many of the residents, particularly the property owners north of the highway. Homes were beginning to take a strong foothold along that

stretch, marring the clean approach to the three churches. The question was asked, "If homes can root there, can business be far behind?" Once again, the passage of a bond issue was the answer. The land had been saved, deeded to the city for park purposes forevermore.

"Beverly Gardens," as the newly landscaped section came to be known (many oldtimers refer to it as "the 80-foot strip"), soon became a focal point within the community—and perhaps the most outstanding feature in what was to become an extensive park system. Extending for 23 blocks, it spanned the entire two-mile length of Beverly Hills. Through the center ran a promenade, ten feet wide, bordered with weeping evergreen elms, beds of rare flowers, magnificent rose gardens, cactus beds, benches, pergolas and lily ponds. It was landscaped to the minutest detail, despite the country's money problems. But as one magazine of the times reported, "Beverly Hills is a town of great wealth and can well afford to indulge in such satisfying accoutrements."

Lily pond on Santa Monica Boulevard between Canon and Beverly Drives, 1929.

Rose garden in the park,
between Maple and Elm Drives.

Vined arbor, right, between Carmelita Avenue and Trenton Drive. Below, wooded path along Santa Monica Boulevard.

Fountain at east end of Beverly Gardens.

181

The cactus garden, running the width of the entire block between
Bedford and Camden Drives, contains one of the largest
collections in the world.

Of all the famous sights in Beverly Hills, the most memorable and, undoubtedly, the most seen over the years is the electric fountain at the intersection of Wilshire and Santa Monica Boulevards. The "crowning jewel" in the development of Beverly Gardens, it was erected at a cost of $22,000.

With its ever-changing combinations of water jets and colored lights, the fountain drew immediate praise. The figure topping the center column is symbolic of an Indian rain-prayer, while the frieze surrounding the base, executed by Merrel Gage, depicts the early history of California. Architect Ralph Flewelling is responsible for the overall design. Much of the credit for bringing the fountain to the much-traveled crossroads belongs to Mrs. Elizabeth Fraser Lloyd, Harold Lloyd's mother, who was active in the project and in civic affairs.

Except for periods of civil emergency, the fountain has operated to the delight of millions of passersby almost daily since its installation.

While Beverly Gardens, with its prime location along the two main highways, received the greatest notoriety, three other parks on the outer edges of the city were immensely popular. Installed in the late 20s, Roxbury, LaCienega and Coldwater Canyon Parks were more isolated and, therefore, catered to the relaxing and recreational needs of the community. Each had its special attractions and its own beauty.

Quiet lily ponds, wandering streams and picturesque bridges characterized the sprawling park in Coldwater Canyon.

The magnificent tiered fountain in Coldwater Canyon Park was removed around 1960 when the Los Angeles County Flood Control District installed a storm drain and catch basin. The entire park was then relandscaped to include a children's play area (above) as well as a jogging track around the old fountain site.

In 1935, a major magazine wrote,
"The Municipal Pool in Beverly Hills'
LaCienega Park is a luxury rather than
a necessity, for the 'Hometown of the
Movies' has the most equable of
climates. It is an accommodation,
however, for those youngsters who
like to go around the corner, as it
were, for their daily dip instead of the
few miles to the nearby sparkling
Pacific." The pool opened in 1929.

Roxbury Park, on Olympic Boulevard, is the hub of community activities, housing the Beverly Hills Recreational Center, the Senior Citizen Center and the Lawn Bowling Club, among others. The Lawn Bowling Club, whose membership includes many leading and longtime residents, was founded in 1926 on a vacant lot in the business district. One of the many competitive games held annually is the Walt Disney Masters Singles in honor of the great showman, who was a member. Roxbury Park, like Coldwater Canyon Park, was relandscaped after flood control work in the early 60s. Opposite, the putting green, mid-30s.

ROXBURY
MEMORIAL PARK
CITY OF BEVERLY HILLS

The two Santa Monica Boulevards at the Wilshire intersection, 1932. An Associated gas station is located at "The Point." Below it, the start of the Beverly Hills Nursery. A portion of the then new Beverly Gardens Park can be seen from this air view.

Looking west along Wilshire Boulevard, 1931. Golfing great Bobby Jones, in "Chip Shots," and Constance Bennett, in "Born to Love," were on the screen at Warner's Beverly. The street lights, of special design when installed in the mid-20s, became a center of controversy in the 50s when replaced by modern mercury vapor fixtures. Note the double-deck bus.

193

Beverly Hills City Hall, 1974.

Since incorporation, Beverly Hills directed its city government from rented quarters in various parts of town. In 1930, however, despite the rumblings of hard times, land was purchased from the Pacific Electric Railway for the start of a new civic center. Construction contracts for the City Hall were awarded in July, 1931, and the building that now houses the city government was dedicated a year later. Opposite page, workmen add finishing touches to terrace entryway prior to opening.

In 1921, when the newly appointed Fire Chief had been at his job only two days, a blaze
was reported in a house on Maple Drive. Of the two men in the department, one was on
vacation and the other was on night duty—and the Chief had no idea where Maple was.
He grabbed the janitor, cranked up the truck and together they found the fire and brought
it under control. The Beverly Hills Fire Department has undergone many changes since the
early days when it, and the Police Department, shared headquarters in the room of a
private home. In 1925, the Fire Department came into being as a separate organization and
in late 1932 a spacious new station adjoining City Hall was completed. Today, with a crew
of over 100 firemen, the Beverly Hills Fire Department not only fights fires but also
conducts a highly effective fire prevention program, using the latest fire-fighting equipment
and maintaining an elaborate communications system. To its credit, Beverly Hills has
experienced no major fires in its history.

The canyons of Beverly Hills: Benedict Canyon (left) showing a portion of the
Harold Lloyd estate, Greenacres, at far left center. Above, Franklin Canyon
reservoir is circled by Coldwater Canyon and Beverly Drives, 1933.

CHANGES

As the movie industry boomed and Beverly
Hills blossomed with stars and mansions, the
Beverly Hills Hotel found itself in the middle
of America's richest village. Under Mrs. Margaret Anderson's guidance, it became a center
for community activities where church services
were held, free silent movies were shown, and
society gathered. Tournaments, shows and
competitions were staged near the front entrance (an 18-hole miniature golf course was
only a few feet away) and as the "Roaring 20s"
hit its stride, the atmosphere lightened with the
times. But the hotel was about to lose a friend
—and the nation, its spark.

In 1928, Mrs. Anderson sold the hotel to a
corporation. A year later, the country was hit
by the Depression. When the hotel closed its
doors, people were shocked. It *had* to survive.
After all, before there was Beverly Hills, there
was the Beverly Hills Hotel. But the doors
were to remain closed for several years.

By the time the hotel reopened in late 1933, it
had been redecorated with the latest furnishings and conveniences, and the former children's dining room had been transformed into a
bar. Much fanfare accompanied the reopening,
the start of a new era. But the real savior was
waiting in the wings, and its greatest success
was still years away.

*Jocko, the monkey, entertains youngsters
at an Easter party on the front lawn of
the Beverly Hills Hotel, 1928.*

A portion of the main lobby, 30s-style. Today, the fireplace burns continually, symbolic of the warmth and hospitality provided the weary travelers by the Franciscan padres in mission days.

Despite the new look to the former children's dining room, times were bad. Management felt that to lure more of the wealthy townsfolk, people like Darryl Zanuck, Walter Wanger and Will Rogers, who were known to "water up" after chukkers, an appealing name was needed. They decided to call it the Polo Lounge.

THE LETTER

In 1928, a committee was appointed and action started to secure a post office for Beverly Hills. Two of the committeemen, members of the Chamber of Commerce, appeared before the Appropriations Committee in Washington and through their efforts an offer was made to provide $85,000—which the city rejected as insufficient. The hoped-for new post office building appeared doomed. Then Will Rogers stepped in. In 1930, he wrote the following letter to Secretary of the Treasury Andrew Mellon (the original copy remains today with the Mellon family and is considered a prize piece of political literature): "Dear Mr. Mellon—This will introduce to you Mr. Lon Haddock of Beverly Hills, California. It seems that you owe us $250,000 to build a post office and they can't get the dough out of you, and I told them that I knew you and that you

weren't that kind of fellow at heart. So in place of suing you, why, he is going back there and see if he can't jar you lose from it. We are getting a lot of mail out here now, and they are handling it in a tent. It is mostly circulars from Washington with speeches on prosperity, but it makes awful good reading while waiting for the foreclosure . . . By the way, if some town don't call for their post office money, why lay it aside for Claremore, Oklahoma. We don't get no mail, but might if we had a post office. Hope the budget balances. Will Rogers"

Washington officials appropriated $300,000 and the post office was built. An elaborate dedication, with a week-long "City Salute," was held on April 28, 1934.

O.N. Beasley and his Beverly Hills National Bank made national headlines during the Depression. When Franklin D. Roosevelt ordered the banks closed at the beginning of his term as President, Beasley refused because his bank was solvent. The bank, shown in 1934 (left) was located at the corner of Camden Drive and Little Santa Monica Boulevard.

RESIDENCES

*The home of
actor Wallace Beery.*

The home of actress Jean Harlow.

Left, home of actress Lupe Valez.

The estate of long-time resident Mrs. Virginia Robinson, of the J.W. Robinson department store chain.

Garden,
Harvey Mudd estate.

By 1936, radio station KMPC had long been a fixture along Wilshire Boulevard, its tower one of the most imposing structures in the city. Having to share its mission-style headquarters with a gas station, however, left little room for growth; within seven years (1943), the "station of the stars," as it was known, shifted its operation to Hollywood. The building, extensively remodeled, later became the annex for Saks Fifth Avenue.

The northwest corner of Doheny Drive and Olympic Boulevard, 1936.

Thirty-Two Pages

Beverly Hills Fire Department OX 2323
Police and Ambulance OX 6181

THE BEVERLY HILLS CITIZEN

OFFICIAL PAPER OF BEVERLY HILLS

In the early 20s, despite its discovery by the stars and the ensuing real estate boom, the little city was developing a complex. No real champion had emerged to publicize and fight for the necessities created by the sudden growth. A new city hall was needed . . . a library . . . street improvements . . . transportation . . . additional school facilities . . . on and on. To make matters worse, the metropolitan newspapers were virtually ignoring the developments that had taken place within the city and of which the residents were understandably proud.

In May of 1923 two things happened to brighten that picture: Beverly Hills got its own "publicist"—and a newspaper. Perhaps no two organizations played a more important part in developing community consciousness and pride than the Chamber of Commerce and the *Beverly Hills Citizen.*

The history of both organizatoins paralleled the history and growth of the city and, though no longer operating, the *Citizen* still holds a fond place in the residents' hearts. It started on a small scale, as a magazine, later expanding to a full-size weekly newspaper. From the beginning it carried a legend on its masthead acknow-

ledging its hometown roots. And as the paper strengthened its position and increased frequency (it ultimately became a daily), it acquired companion publications and, with each step, larger quarters. In later years, the *Citizen* changed names almost as frequently as it changed hands, although the Will Rogers family owned it for 17 years. During its time, however, the *Beverly Hills Citizen* was "the voice" of the city and a dominant factor in its development.

Beverly Hills had another publication of note, thanks to Charlie Chaplin. In the late 20s, nationally known journalist Rob Wagner decided to publish a weekly paper in a remote desert town "just for the fun of it," planning to pepper it with fictional stories about imaginary characters. Friend Chaplin offered him $30,000 to start the paper on one condition, that he would remain in Beverly Hills where he wouldn't have to invent stories or characters. Wagner refused the money, wanting to make a go of it on his own, but he did stay to publish a magazine, *Script,* filling it with stories written by friends and contemporaries. The first issue, dated February 16, 1929, created little stir. But during its nearly 20 years of publication, *Script* became a literary gem, receiving national attention and acclaim.

214

Illustration from 1937 issue announcing the Citizen's new plant on North Canon Drive. The building, still standing, has since been remodeled and is known today as The Courtyard.

First Church of Christ, Scientist, Beverly Hills, is a branch of The Mother Church, The First Church of Christ, Scientist, in Boston. The original local group (Society) held its first services in a rented Masonic Hall in October, 1923. By 1928, it was recognized by The Mother Church and incorporated in September. That same year, on a portion of the current site on South Rexford Drive, a large California-style cottage became the first church building. In 1937, the cornerstone was laid for the present church structure. Completed in March, 1938, the church has since received a Beautification Award for its extensive landscaping and grounds.

Right, the First Church of Christ, Scientist, Beverly Hills today.

ADVERTISING

Temple Emanuel, Beverly Hills' only Reform Temple, was founded in 1938 and dedicated to serve the spiritual, religious and educational needs of its congregation. The Temple Sanctuary on Clark Drive, built in 1954, houses the Rabbi Harrison Chapel, a nursery school, bridal room, an auditorium, the Board of Directors' Room, and the Rabbinical offices. Across the street, on Burton Way, is the Temple's modern, two-story religious school building containing an amphitheater auditorium, an extensive Judaic library, two meeting halls, and executive offices.

Temple Emanuel of Beverly Hills.

THE SIX MILLION

Memorial Sculpture at Temple Emanuel Sanctuary.

Forecourt of the Sanctuary.

*Temple Emanuel's
modern, two-story
religious school building.*

THE FORTIES

War and Europe seemed far away in 1940. The following year was a different story. With the attack on Pearl Harbor, Beverly Hills plunged into the fight. Two draft boards were opened, the Red Cross headquartered in City Hall tower, a USO unit was organized. The Beverly Wilshire Hotel was designated as the official air raid shelter. "Victory Gardens" were started on empty lots, even along Wilshire Boulevard, with special water rates adopted for those participating in the program. The city's War Bond drives were instrumental in raising enormous sums of cash (composer Jimmy McHugh personally raised over $28 million and was cited by President Truman). At war's end, the Christmas lights again sparkled and sixty stores began a new trend by staying open on Monday evenings. One realtor noted that property values had not yet peaked when a 100-foot lot sold for $6,000. Six months later it resold for $26,000. Parking began to be a problem and Howard Hughes made news by crashing his huge plane into a private residence on Whittier Drive. As the decade came to a close, Beverly Hills led the state in a 10-year jump in retail sales—and had the lowest tax rate.

Mt. Calvary Lutheran Church, an affiliate of the Southern California District of the Lutheran Church, Missouri Synod, acquired its present site on South Beverly Drive in April, 1941. Following its inaugural service seven months earlier, the church dedicated the first building (a chapel-parish hall unit) on Sunday, December 21, 1941. Additional property was purchased in 1944 and in late 1947 the congregation dedicated a greatly enlarged parish hall and chapel. Growth continued to the point where even larger facilities were necessary. In April, 1955, groundbreaking ceremonies were held for an extensive new sanctuary, dedicated on September 23, 1956.

5TH WAR LOAN

Back the Attack! - BUY MORE THAN BEFORE

During World War II, registration desks manned by service personnel were commonplace—even in the lobby of the Beverly Hills Hotel.

A War Bond drive, netting $1.7 million, resulted in the sponsorship of a superfortress, the "City of Beverly Hills," and a flying fortress, the "Spirit of Beverly Hills." Per capita bond sales were the highest in the nation; over $100 million worth were sold in a city of only 30,000 people.

RESIDENCES

Above, the home of actress Olivia de Havilland; left, Paulette Goddard.

Right, the home of actor Thomas Mitchell; below, Columbia Pictures chief, Harry Cohn.

Above, the residence of restaurateur Michael Romanoff; left, actress Maria Montez.

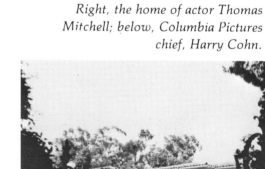

Wilshire Boulevard, looking west, from Hamilton Drive on the eastern edge of the city, then (1940s) and now. The building at far left (above) is the dramatic Great Western Savings Center, the first elliptically shaped building in western America.

Following the war, the name establishments took an even stronger foothold in the business community. It was only the beginning.

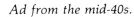

Adrian

P R E S E N T S

HIS DISTINGUISHED

COLLECTION FOR FALL

YOUR INSPECTION

IS INVITED

233 NORTH BEVERLY DRIVE · BEVERLY HILLS

North on Beverly Drive from Wilshire Boulevard, 1947. The building in the left center of photo was opened in 1934 as a Victor Hugo Restaurant. Later, it was the headquarters for internationally famous designer, Adrian, as well as the first home of Robinson's Beverly.

In the late 1940s, Metro-Goldwyn-Mayer studios established an FM radio station (KMGM) on a mountaintop high above Beverly Hills, primarily as an outlet to promote its own product. Beverly Hills record store owner A. Arthur Crawford bought the station in 1952, revamped the programming along classical lines and boosted its power from 50,000 to 75,000 watts, making KCBH (the new call letters) one of the most powerful stations in Southern California. In 1970, Abel Communications, Inc. purchased the facilities and the station became known as KJOI. Today, with its "beautiful music" format, KJOI ranks in the top ten among all stations in Los Angeles—and the once isolated retreat at the top of the mountain has become a thriving, mini-communications center.

The mountaintop site of today's KJOI, as it looked in the early days.

The southeast corner of Wilshire and Robertson Boulevards, late 1940s.

Romanoff's, on South Rodeo Drive, was one of Beverly
Hill's most famous celebrity restaurants during the
post-war days. Your host: the legendary "Prince" Michael
Romanoff

THE AWAKENING

As the Thirties were coming to an end, the downtown Los Angeles and mid-Wilshire hotels had become the centers of Southland social life, and the aging Beverly Hills Hotel had fallen on hard times. Earlier attempts to revive its former stature had failed. The younger crowd stayed away and it attracted only a sedate, mature clientele. Ultimately, the hotel fell into receivership.

The hotel's trustee, Bank of America, had working for it at the time a young vice-president named Hernando Courtright. Rounding up a number of investors, he bought the hotel and planned sweeping changes that included major remodeling of the existing structure, a new wing, and a tradition of impeccable service. The public responded. The hotel not only "came back" but it was elevated to a status it had never attained before. Suddenly, the Beverly Hills Hotel had become the residence of the elite: royalty, tycoons, celebrities, leaders from all walks of life.

The Beverly Hills Hotel dedicates its new $1.5 million wing in 1949.

SPENCE

Under Hernando Courtright's leadership,
the Beverly Hills Hotel became one of the
most prestigious in the world.

THE FIFTIES

Post-war growth continued at a phenomenal pace. Business hit an all-time high with bank debits equaling those of a city five times its size; per capita sales topped the nation with $3,604 per person. The population numbered approximately 30,000 and only a handful of vacant residential lots remained. Marion Davies' estate on Lexington Road, known as "the second San Simeon," was being subdivided. The former Walter G. McCarty estate, later occupied by the Duke and Duchess of Windsor, was being leveled. To further ease the situation, a mountain was literally reshaped. Large eastern corporations and establishments continued the swing westward, opening offices in Beverly Hills. Among them, Time, Life & Fortune. Parking meters were installed in the business "triangle" (the first month's take returned over $10,000) and Marie Sleuth, William Powell's dog, was abducted. Corinne Griffith began construction on the last corner building at the intersection of Beverly Drive and Charleville, completing her ownership of all four corners and becoming one of only three people in the country to have such holdings. The city, with its borders bulging, had seemingly filled to capacity.

Beverly Hills, north from Pico Boulevard, 1953.
(Beverly and Beverwill Drives cut vertically
through center of photo.)

In late 1950, the new Beverly Hills YMCA building opened as "a boost for the youngsters of the community." It was constructed at a cost of $250,000 on the west side of town.

In 1950, Gloria Swanson officiated at a ceremony marking completion of the installation of nearly 900 new street signs, held at the corner of Crescent Drive and Sunset Boulevard where Miss Swanson once owned one of the first celebrity homes in the area. The new signs, in a reversal of the customary white on black, were adopted for legibility and maintenance.

Sunset Park, the oldest park in the city, was officially renamed Will Rogers Park in 1952.

The Frank Lloyd Wright building on North Rodeo Drive was one of the last that the master architect designed. It was completed in 1953.

With great fanfare, J.W. Robinson's opened its showplace on February 11, 1952. For some time, it seemed somewhat isolated on the western edge of the city. It wasn't until Conrad Hilton stepped in to fill the wide open spaces of "The Point" that Robinson's Beverly seemed as close as it really was.

The Beth Jacob Congregation, Beverly Hills' only Orthodox Synagogue, was organized in the West Adams area of Los Angeles in 1928; its school then known as the West Adams Community School. In 1954, the Congregation moved to its present location on Olympic Boulevard. Today, the educational program of Beth Jacob includes sponsorship of the Hillel Hebrew Academy.

The Beth Jacob Congregation of Beverly Hills.

Beverly Hills gained added luster as established "favorites" were joined by newcomers.

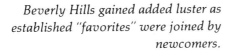

Wilshire Boulevard at night, ca 1955.

World-famous Restaurant Row on La Cienega Boulevard.

ADVERTISING

260

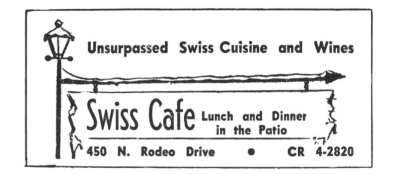

Beverly Hills' Moorish showhouse, the Beverly Theater, held its gala grand opening on Monday, May 18, 1925, before a star-studded hometown audience. Reported a Southland newspaper, "The theater itself, one of the most beautiful in all of Southern California, caused ripples of joyful appreciation throughout the capacity crowd. At last Beverly Hills, home of the movie folks, has its own home for their productions." Director Fred Niblo, emcee of the event, commented, "We've waited long for you and now you're here. We hope you will always show us the good, clean, higher type of pictures." The first feature shown was First National Pictures' "I Want My Man," starring Milton Sills and Doris Kenyon. Also on the program was a filmed tour through the local movie stars' homes.

The controversial 1955 film, "The Man With The Golden Arm," returned the Beverly Theater to first-run status after a number of years. NBC announcer-emcee Hy Averback (left) greets Frank Sinatra, Dorothy Dandridge and Judy Garland on their arrival at the theater.

In 1950, Conrad Hilton stunned the local scene by filing an application for a $17 million hotel, to be built on the former site of the Beverly Hills Nursery—and since its departure by a "sock 'em" golf practice range. Three years later, ground was broken for the flagship hotel of the world-wide Hilton chain.

In August, 1955, the Beverly Hilton Hotel, with a time capsule sealed in its cornerstone, opened to great acclaim. Located at the crossroads of two of the world's most traveled thoroughfares, it immediately became a major addition to the city and a mecca for distinguished clientele.

The Beverly Hilton Hotel, located at the busy intersection of Santa Monica and Wilshire Boulevards.

Above, original drawing for "proposed" Beverly Hilton Hotel emphasizes the dramatic location. Left, situated at the hotel's easternmost point, famed Trader Vic's offers Polynesian cuisine in a South Seas atmosphere.

The tropical entry welcomes guests from all over the world.

Conrad N. Hilton (right), chairman of the board, Hilton Hotels Corporation, and former hotel general manager Robert Groves check finishing touches to the multi-story Fountain Lanai addition. The new wing opened in 1967.

The Beverly Hilton boasts one of the most popular gourmet dining spots in the city, L'Escoffier. It's rooftop setting affords a spectacular panoramic view.

269

THE DOHENY RANCH

In the 1920s, the historic Doheny Ranch consisted of 410 rolling acres and a castle-like mansion named Greystone. Thirty years later, Greystone remained a fortress overlooking Beverly Hills and the entire Los Angeles basin, from the mountains to the sea. But the once sprawling croplands had become near-priceless real estate and the ranch itself the scene of one of the largest earth moving operations in the history of Southern California—the start of the world's most expensive subdivision, Trousdale Estates. There, 539 fabulous homesites, ranging in size from 20,000 square feet to four acres, were to ride the side of the Santa Monica Mountains, priced (both property and homes) from only $150,000 to $2 million.

February, 1932—The Doheny Ranch five years after completion of Greystone Mansion, seen at lower left.

May, 1960—Same view with many changes as residential view sites are being carved out of the hills.

Grading a now-famous crossroads: Drury Lane and Hillcrest Road, 1955.

*August, 1955—The work has begun. Looking north from near Doheny Road; the
row of palm trees follow what is now Hillcrest Road.*

. . . building pads
for Trousdale Estates

View toward Hollywood from Trousdale Estates.

In 1917, at least eight cars a day passed through the town of Beverly Hills. Feeling threatened by this problem, the Trustees decided they needed a motor police officer and tabbed the only man in town who could ride a motorcycle, a famed jockey on the leading tracks of the country. With those qualifications, Charlie Blair was appointed City Marshall. Beverly Hills had no jail so culprits receiving a sentence were taken to the Blair house where they were given food and lodging. "Suspicious characters" were trundled aboard the Pacific Electric car, fare paid, with the conductor instructed to keep them from disembarking before reaching Los Angeles—or at least until they had passed the city limits where a sign warned "Burglars and Robbers—Stay Out!"

By 1937, the Beverly Hills Police Department was recognized by government officials as being "without equal in the country." In 1949, all persons charged with robbery, burglary and auto thefts during the year were found guilty. One reporter labeled it "a remarkable piece of police work"—not to mention a strong deterrent against future acts. The solid reputation of the department has continued. Probably no one, any place, is more secure than in Beverly Hills. Patrols are constantly on the alert. "They are everywhere," one resident noted, "and, if not, close to it."

In 1957, Beverly Hills High School marked its 30th anniversary. Those years saw continued expansion activities, including added classroom facilities, a new athletic field, and a $120,000 swimming pool and gymnasium with a unique pool cover to convert the pool area to basketball use.

Walter G. McCarty, builder of the imposing Beverly Wilshire Hotel, envisioned a grand apartment-hotel catering exclusively to the carriage trade. Constructed on a choice parcel of his land, a portion of which was the Beverly Hills Speedway, the building and sweeping lawns consumed an entire block, from Wilshire south to Charleville. With the growth and development of the surrounding area, the open spaces began to disappear. Unlike its rival across town, the hotel enhanced its enviable reputation.

Walter McCarty's ownership lasted 17 years. In 1945, Arnold S. Kirkeby purchased the hotel. Under his guidance, and that of Evelyn Sharp who followed (1957-1962), the Beverly Wilshire assumed an increasingly commercial character. World War II had just ended; times were good. Kirkeby added a supper club and introduced Kay Thompson and the Williams Brothers. Matt Dennis appeared at the piano in the Brazilian Room, while Ted Fio Rito entertained in the Mayfair Room. The Copa Club and Pool went in and the doors were open to anyone in the neighborhood who wanted to join. A drug store, Milton F. Kreiss, on the Rodeo-Wilshire corner became an all-night gathering spot. Tennis championships were held and attracted the top stars of the day (Bobby Riggs, Don Budge and the two "Panchos," Gonzales and Segura) for purses of up to $5,000. Eventually, the increased activity took its toll and the hotel began to lose its exclusivity. The bloom had suddenly faded. It seemed that only a miracle (or miracle man) could restore the Beverly Wilshire to its rightful status.

The Beverly Wilshire's famous Copa Club and Pool. The tennis court disappeared in the late 50s for parking; the pool in the late 60s.

RESIDENCES

The residences of Agnes Moorehead (above) and Rex Harrison (left).

Left, the home of Elizabeth Taylor and Michael Todd.

The home of Lana Turner.

Right, the residence of Rita Hayworth and Ali Kahn.

Clockwise, the homes of Clifton Webb, George Burns and Gracie Allen, Ronald Colman and Edgar Bergen.

Left, the residence of James Roosevelt.

THE SIXTIES

It was a time to remember. Beverly Hills had come of age and paused to celebrate its 50th anniversary. But the revelers could barely compete with the continuing roar of the construction corps along the city's central core. The boundaries may have felt the strain of the building boom but the skies hadn't been touched. Beverly Hills was moving ahead—and up. Financial institutions had "discovered" the city *en masse*; more than ten times the norm for a city its size was establish-

ing headquarters or branches. Too, the village-like side streets, populated by quaint dress and gift shops, (pioneers of the boutique and small specialty merchandising which set a national trend), were undergoing not-so-subtle changes. Internationally famous names were moving in at a heady rate, now replacing many of the old favorites. Unlike the puffery of the 30s, Beverly Hills had indeed arrived as the indisputable center of prestige shopping.

A ride down Rodeo Drive during the 20s was often at a slow, relaxing pace. Four decades later, the tempo had quickened considerably.

Silver Anniversary Celebration in 1939 was attended by a number of personalities, including (l-r): Eddie Cantor, Mr. and Mrs. Fred Niblo, Conrad Nagle and (not shown) Billie Burke, Harold Lloyd, Robert Young, Frank Morgan and Mrs. Will Rogers.

Planting the newly developed "Beverly Hills Rose."

Beverly Hills' two milestone anniversaries (the 25th in 1939; the 50th in 1964) were marked by a number of memorable events. Of national importance was a star-studded 90-minute color spectacular on NBC television, hosted by Art Linkletter in 1964. Dozens of top entertainment personalities and local dignitaries were featured along with tours of the famous homes and shopping spots.

298

The home of Mrs. Virginia Robinson was the scene of the 50th Anniversary Press Party on January 14, 1964 where composers Jimmy McHugh (seated) and Ned Washington (right) previewed "The Wonderful World of Beverly Hills," their salute to the city. The Beverly Wilshire's Hernando Courtright (third from right) is among civic leaders gathered around the piano.

RESIDENCES

The homes of (right, above) Director Vincent Minnelli and (below) Jimmy Durante.
Opposite page: Rosalind Russell and Fred Brisson.

301

The residence of composer-conductor Johnny Green.

Julie Andrews and Blake Edwards.

Jack Benny and Mary Livingston.

Oscar Levant

George Murphy

Phil Silvers

Fredric March and Florence Eldridge

The first public library was established in Beverly Hills in 1914 as a branch of the Los Angeles County Library. Located in the old Coldwater Schoolhouse, it remained there until 1922 when it moved to larger quarters on the second floor of a commercial building in town. By 1924, with the growth of the city and the library itself, it was felt that Beverly Hills had sufficient population to support a library of its own. But it was 1929 before the City Council passed an ordinance to that effect. Again, temporary quarters were found until a permanent home could be readied in a wing of the then-new City Hall. There it remained for over 30 years, until the dedication of its very own home on North Rexford Drive on October 10, 1965. Today, in a city of approximately 34,000 population, the Beverly Hills Public Library serves nearly 43,000 registered borrowers.

West on Wilshire from Cañon Drive, 1965.

One of the many magnificient residences along Sunset Boulevard.

In January, 1966, representatives of Beverly Hills and Acapulco met in the Mexican resort town to announce the joining of hands in the Sister City "People-to-People" Program. Like Beverly Hills, Acapulco is a city of dramatic physical beauty, with impressive homes maintained by local and international notables, glamourous hotels, and a thriving tourist industry.

The look of Beverly Hills changed dramatically during the 60s, the result of a furious building boom. From Doheny Drive to the Wilshire-Santa Monica intersection, hardly a block along "the fabulous boulevard" was left untouched.

The Friars Club of California, Inc., incorporated in 1946, is a prestigious social club, consisting of men engaged in the theatrical and professional fields. Known for its good fellowship and entertainment (their "roasts" are legend), the club is equally dedicated to giving support, financial and otherwise, to the underprivileged and to various charitable, worthy movements and causes. The Friars Club Charity Foundation, an independent corporation, was organized in 1956 to carry on many charitable and philanthropic activities. Over the years, millions of dollars have been contributed to various charities.

Originally located in the former Romanoff's Restaurant building on North Rodeo Drive, the club moved to its home on Little Santa Monica Boulevard in 1961.

When concerned residents demonstrated for signals in 1924 it took days to arrange a staged tie-up at the Wilshire-Santa Monica Boulevard intersection. By the 60s, traffic had become a common sight.

The Beverly Hills Tennis Club on North Maple Drive.

Looking down Santa Monica Boulevard, across Wilshire,
toward Hollywood and Los Angeles, 1967.

Looking west from intersection of Wilshire and LaCienega Boulevards (Wilshire runs up center of photo). Santa Monica Bay can be seen in the upper lef corner.

The William Morris
Agency, talent agency for
all phases of the
entertainment world, has
headquartered in Beverly
Hills for over 30 years.

Litton Industries established its headquarters in Beverly Hills in the early 50s. At that time, as a small electronics firm, it employed less than 300 people and, in its first year of operation, recorded sales of $3 million. Today, Litton is a multi-national, multi-product industrial corporation with over 100,000 employees in 27 countries, and sales in the billions of dollars.

In the fall of 1969, Litton moved its entire operation from the original location on Foothill Road to its present corporate headquarters, Litton Industries Plaza, on North Crescent Drive. Comprising three Colonial-style buildings, the Plaza reflects the residential image of its noted surroundings.

Litton Plaza South, newest of the corporate buildings, was completed in late 1969. In keeping with the architectural theme, the interiors were designed in the Georgian-Colonial style and furnished with replicas of the 18th century.

Litton Plaza North was formerly the headquarters of MCA.

Litton Plaza North was built in 1937 as the headquarters for Music Corporation of America (MCA). The architectural design was conceived by Jules Stein, head of MCA, who wanted the building to look as much like a home as possible, while functioning as an office. It's the spot that once controlled the pulse of the entertainment industry as many of the top stars, writers, directors and producers were under its wing. Considerable Hollywood folklore is associated with the former MCA site, as well as numerous fallacies, particularly one concerning its famous circular twin staircases in the main lobby. (Scarlett O'Hara did not tumble from its height in "Gone With The Wind".)

The Beverly Hills landmark was purchased by Litton Industries in 1964.

The lamps of the Plaza once lighted the streets of Copenhagen, Denmark.

The Plaza contains a magnificent 30-foot high Tuscan colonnade. At its base, centered within a large fountain pool, is a 100-year-old bronze statue of the god Neptune. Dividing the corridor of the Plaza, leading to the fountain, are a series of blue reflection pools.

The original Beverly Hills headquarters for Litton Industries on Foothill Road, ca 1958.

THE SEVENTIES

Beverly Hills was first and foremost a residential community. Later, it gained fame for its elegant shops. Today, it boasts a new reputation: Wall Street of the West. While most communities would happily settle for any one of the three, residents are determined to retain the highly residential character of their city.

Bevery Hills is not large. Its population is relatively small. The number of dwelling units, single and multiple family, is only around 15,000. When the last office building has emptied in late afternoon, and the cars and buses carry their passengers away (over 100,000 people work in the city, the vast majority crossing its limits daily), Beverly Hills returns to its normal, exclusive status. New terms have crept into modern-day conversations: traffic flow, height and density, freeway access. Beverly Hills is not without its problems —some new, some continuing—but it never was. Somehow, it has always found the answers—in consummate style.

Gateway Lodge, off the Sunset Boulevard curve on the western edge of the city, has been a landmark for motorists for years. Brown and yellow "shields" (left photo) are posted on the outer limits of most major thoroughfares.

Beverly Hills Municipal Court, Alpine Drive and Burton Way, was dedicated in 1970.

A section of Lexington Road is landscaped with nearly 250 towering Canary Island pines.

When Hernando Courtright moved to the Beverly Hills Hotel, at a rather early point in his career, he was known primarily as a banker. By 1962, his reputation had broadened considerably. He had established himself as a host, entertainer, gourmet, horseman, innkeeper and developer. But, above all, a *miracle worker*. Though away from the hotel business since 1954, he had not been inactive, having served as the first president of Century City, the 260-acre high-rise development flanking the west side of Beverly Hills.

Like the Beverly Hills Hotel in the 30s, the once-prestigious Beverly Wilshire was showing signs of age —and was badly in need of a knowledgeable guiding hand. With the arrival of Hernando Courtright, its destiny seemed assured. Determined to restore the

The dazzling entry to the Beverly Wilshire Hotel, "El Camino Real," a nostalgic reminder of California's romantic past.

The canopied Wilshire Boulevard entrance to the hotel.

The Beverly Wilshire's Hernando Courtright.

bloom to the cheeks of the Grand Dame, he wasted no time by creating a master plan. First, he introduced new dining facilities and made the hotel a leading center for gourmets. He followed by rejuvenating the old 10-story building (the giant neon sign on the roof was immediately expendable), embellishing and surpassing the Old World splendor of the original. The success of the new Beverly Wilshire Hotel led to Phase II: erection of a magnificent $20 million, 12-story addition.

The 250-room Beverly Wing opened in late 1971 to world-wide acclaim, the first hotel in America to be awarded the Grand Luxe hallmark, until then granted only to Europe's finest palace-inns, not only for its beauty and comfort but for the excellence of its cuisine and personalized service as well. Distinguished by its decor (custom-designed around various periods in California history), its masterful craftsmanship, and by the selection of superb domestic and imported materials, the Beverly Wilshire is a triumph. Says famed architect Charles Luckman, "No one builds palaces like this any more, much less hotels."

Reception area of the main lobby reflects the hotel's return to elegance.

Right, gaslights and fountains, the Mediterranean atmosphere of the colorful pool-patio. Below, the elegant two-story townhouse suites feature 20-foot ceilings and interior staircases.

Gaslights at entry to "El Camino Real" were imported from Scotland's Edinburgh Castle.

Curving staircase, with classic wrought iron grillwork, is flanked by varicolored columns of Tinos Vert marble.

North on Beverly Drive from Olympic Boulevard.

South on Crescent Drive from Lexington Road.

...FAMOUS PLACES

East on Sunset Boulevard from Whittier Drive, 1972.

With Hernando Courtright's departure from the Beverly Hills Hotel in the early 50s, there were some fears the "The Pink Palace" on Sunset Boulevard would once again slide from its lofty position, a spot to which Courtright himself had personally elevated it during his command. In 1954, the Beverly Hills Hotel Corporation, headed by New York lawyer and financier Ben Silberstein, took control. From the start, it was obvious that the hotel's impeccable service and style would be sedulously maintained.

Secluded within 16 acres of flowering gardens and towering palms, in an atmosphere of understated elegance, the hotel attracts a royal registry. The Astors, Vanderbilts, Fords and Firestones have stayed there—as have the Rockefellers, duPonts and Kennedys. The Polo Lounge, hub of the hotel, has served them all, from Barrymore, Dietrich and Fields to Monroe, Taylor and Sinatra. The Sand and Pool Club entertains the same cast of beautiful people who, in other seasons, may be found in Acapulco, St. Moritz or the Cote d'Azur. And the bungalows, favorite hideaways since the earliest days, are home to the giants of all professions.

The Beverly Hills Hotel today ranks as one of the last remaining bastions of gracious innkeeping, perpetuating a tradition that *is* Beverly Hills.

The sweeping approach to the Beverly Hills Hotel.

Through the years, the bungalows of the
Beverly Hills Hotel have held a special
attraction, offering the seclusion of a
private residence. The guest list has
included the Duke and Duchess of
Windsor, Prince and Princess Rainier of
Monaco, and Queen Juliana of the
Netherlands.

The Polo Patio, where guests may enjoy al fresco dining in a lush Italian-style garden. Nearby, the Polo Lounge, the world's most glamorous (and enduring) bar. It has played host to the greatest names from all walks of life, as well as the aspiring.

The Beverly Hills Hotel pool, an enormous turquoise lagoon in its tropical setting. Katharine Hepburn is said to have executed a flawless back-flip, fully clothed, from the diving board following a tennis lesson.

Beverly Hills street scene: Hartford Way and Lexington Road are crowded with studio trailers and equipment as road sign alerts residents and passersby to location shooting for new motion picture. Crews from Universal Pictures studios have transformed the grounds of the former Burton Green estate into a party setting for the film "Gable and Lombard."

RESIDENCES

The homes of (above) Debbie Reynolds and (below) Dinah Shore.

Left, the home of Paul Newman and Joanne Woodward.

The residences of (above) Carol Burnett
and Joe Hamilton and (right) Dorothy
McGuire. Opposite page, Jimmy
Stewart.

358

Right, the home of Steve Lawrence and Edie Gorme; (below, left) Gene Kelly and (below right) Ann Rutherford and William Dozier.

Left, the residence of Lucille Ball and Gary Morton.

What started on a rather small scale in the early 70s evolved into a "Blockbusting Beverly Hills Block Party" in 1975. On the evening of May 25, the giant benefit raised $250,000 for "The Concern Foundation" for Cancer Research with the help of such luminaries as Andy Williams, Roger Miller, Liza Minnelli, Lily Tomlin and Lorna Luft. Above, setting up on Rodeo Drive for the evening's festivities.

362

New home of the Academy of Motion Picture Arts and Sciences on Wilshire Boulevard. For nearly 20 years, from 1946 until mid-1975, the Academy occupied the former Marquis Theater building on Melrose Avenue in West Hollywood. The new headquarters houses all offices, its renowned Margaret Herrick Library, and theater facilities.

Wilshire Boulevard,
1975 . . .

*and the architecture
that makes it so unique . . .*

365

Manufacturers Bank Building

Executive Life Insurance Company

United California Bank

Perpetual Savings & Loan Association

Glendale Federal Savings
& Loan Association

City National Bank

The Hongkong Bank of California

Ahmanson Bank & Trust Company

Great Western Savings Center

EPILOGUE

In 1912, Beverly Hills was a name, a hotel and a handful of houses surrounded by a spreading city. But more than anything, it was a dream. Through the years, many giants have walked through the city. Many have stayed to help make that dream come true.

"Don Benito" Wilson and William Workman once built a fence around Rancho El Rodeo de las Aguas to protect their holdings, but it was dismantled for scrap. Douglas Fairbanks once humorously suggested building a wall around the city to preserve its identity, but it never happened. Beverly Hills needs no barrier. It's a world all its own—an incredible, magnificent little civic island. Truly, one of the fabled cities.

IN APPRECIATION

Special thanks to the many individuals who gave so generously of their time, their momentos and, above all, their memories . . . .

Alice Rae Bystrom	Claude V. Meconis
Helen V. Chaplin	John Morosco
Dona Carn	Marjorie Mulholland
Lisa Choeffel	Mary Kay Murray
Sally Cobb	Dolorez Nariman
Paula W. Cohen	Maurene Noble
Mrs. William T. Copenhaver	John Norlander
Police Chief B.L. Cork	Norman A. Pabst
Hernando Courtright	Raymond Page
Harry Donaldson	Carolyn Swarzwald Patterson
Beverly Edwards	Wanda D. Phillips
Jose Garcia	Mrs. Art Pillsbury
Frank Gossett	Audrey Plant
John Glick	Victor Plukas
Dorothy Hardage	Reverend John D. Quinn
Camille Knickerbocker	Liliore Green Rains
Ken Lamb	Karl Schurz
E. Joyce Latta	Phyllis Seaton
Bud Lewis	Mal Sibley
Don Lewis	Ben Silberstein
Willard J. Lewis	Jim Slater
Gordon Levoy	Marvin E. Smith
Jack Linger	Jean Ushnima
Earl Liske	Neil Van Scoten
Gordon Mason	Ralph Wadsworth

INDEX

Abel Communications, Inc., 238
Academy of Motion Picture Arts and Sciences, 64, 363
Acapulco, 310
Adrian, 236
Advertising, 1920s, 134
Advertising, 1930s, 218
Advertising, 1950s, 259
Ah Fong's, 344
Ahmanson Bank & Trust Company, 372
Alhambra, 14
Allen, Gracie, 295
All Saint's Episcopal Church, 108
Alpine Drive, 13, 49, 331
Alta California, 8
Altadena, town of, 169
Amalgamated Oil Company, 23
Ambassador Hotel, 174
American Film Institute, 124
American Legion Post 253, 93, 103
Amestoy, Domingo, 17, 19
Anderson, Mrs. Margaret, 30, 31, 72, 201
Andrews, Julie, 303
Arden, Elizabeth, 256
Armstrong-Schroder Cafe, 172
Associated Oil Company, 24
Averback, Hy, 263

Ball, Lucille, 360
Bank of America, 164
Bank of Italy, 164
Banning, Phineas, 17
Bara, Theda, 84
Barrymore, John, 84
Barthelmess, Richard, 83
Battaglia, 341
Bean-Eaters, 45
Beasley, O.N., 206
Beaver Dam Academy, 24
Bedford Drive, 76, 183
Beery, Wallace, 83, 207

Behrman, S.N., 83
Bellridge Oil Company, 24
Benedict Canyon, 13, 19, 138, 199
Benedict Canyon Drive, 14, 72, 90
Benedict, Edson A., 19
Benedict, Pierce, 19
Bennett, Constance, 193
Benny, Jack, 158, 303
Bergen, Edgar, 295
Berkeley Hall School, 100
Beth Jacob Congregation, 255
Betiller, Francis V., 153
Beverly Boulevard, 96
Beverly Drive, 26, 42, 45, 54, 56, 67, 71, 93, 136, 157, 163, 164, 167, 179, 199, 227, 236, 246, 339
Beverly Farms, Massachusettes, 26
Beverly Gardens, 179-185, 193
Beverly Hills
—Block Party, 362
—Board of Trustees, 47, 113, 285
—Catholic School, 171
—Chamber of Commerce, 96, 157, 159, 164, 204, 214
—Citizen, 214, 215
—City Hall, 71, 194, 197, 226, 307
—Community Church, 105, 169
—Fiftieth Anniversary, 296, 298, 299
—Fire Department, 197
—Grammar School, 52
—High School, 116, 287
—Hotel, 28, 30, 31, 34, 37, 45, 72, 76, 80, 108, 113, 179, 201-203, 229, 242-245, 348-353
—Hotel Corporation, 348
—Municipal Court, 331
—National Bank, 206
—Nursery, 156, 193, 264
—Police Department, 285
—Post Office, 204
—Presbyterian Church, 105
—Public Library, 307
—Recreational Center, 190
—Rose, 298
—Silver Anniversary, 298
—Society Circus, 159
—Speedway, 56, 58, 61, 288
—Tennis Club, 318
—Utility Company, 70, 71
—Women's Club, 14, 90, 91, 96, 116
Beverly Hill Billys, 169
Beverly Hilton Hotel, 156, 264-269

Beverly Rodeo Hotel, 315
Beverly Theater, 134, 218, 262, 263
Beverly Vista Church, 105
Beverly Vista School, 94, 105, 114, 161
Beverly Wilshire Hotel, 154, 163, 226, 288, 332-337
Beverwill Drive, 246
Bishop, Roland P., 50
Bistro, 342
Blair, Charlie, 285
Blum's, 259
Borge, Victor, 158
Bosworth, Hobart, 96
Boy Scouts of America, 157
Bridle Path Association, 72, 96
Brighton Way, 67, 136, 167
Brisson, Fred, 301
Brown, Nacio Herb, 96
Brown Derby, 174-177
Burke, Billie, 298
Burnett, Carol, 358
Burns, George, 295
Burton Way, 26, 220, 331

Cactus garden, 182
Caillet Pharmacy, 135, 172
Cahuenga, townsite, 23
Camden Drive, 108, 183, 206
Cañada de las Aguas Frias, 13
Cañada de los Encinos, 13
Candy Store, 345
Caufield, Charles A., 23
Cañon Drive, 26, 28, 42, 45, 68, 71, 73, 179, 215
Cantor, Eddie, 177, 298
Cantwell, Most Reverend John Joseph, 76
Carillo, José Antonio, 11, 13
Carmelita Avenue, 181
Carroll & Company, 256
Century City, 116, 332
Chamber of Commerce Banquets, 158
Chaplin, Charles, 83, 84, 214
Charleville, 246, 288
Chateau Thierry, 93
Chatterton, Ruth, 87
Chevy Chase Drive, 14, 90, 91
Chief Walker and his Utah band, 14
Church of the Good Shepherd, 76-79, 171
Christmas Nights, 169
City National Bank, 370

"City of Beverly Hills" superfortress, 229
Clark, Henry C., 27
Cobb, Robert H., 174, 176
Cohn, Harry, 230
Coldwater Canyon, 13, 23, 47, 70, 199
Coldwater Canyon Park, 13, 186, 187
Coldwater School District, 23
Coldwater School House, 23, 42, 307
Colman, Ronald, 295
Community Christmas Tree, 169
Concern Foundation, 362
Cook, Wilbur, 26
Copa Club and Pool, 288
Courrèges, 340
Courtright, Hernando, 242, 245, 299, 332, 334, 348
Courtyard, 215
Crawford's Music, 218, 238
Crescent Drive, 26, 27, 31, 39, 42, 45, 90, 248, 322, 339
Crespi, Father Juan, 9

Daisy, 343
Dalton's Restaurant, 258
Dandridge, Dorothy, 263
Daughters of the American Revolution, 14
Davies, Marion, 83, 246
deHavilland, Olivia, 230
De Las Aguas Land Association, 22
DeMille, Cecil B., 17
DeMille, Cecilia Hoyt, 96
Denker, Charles, 22
Dennis, Matt, 288
de Palma, Ralph, 56
de Paolo, Peter, 56
Depression, 163, 164, 201, 206
Derby House, 176
Dias Dorados, 88
Disney Masters Singles, 190
Doheny Drive, 23, 72, 213, 313
Doheny, Edward, 124
Doheny, Edward, Jr., 124
Doheny Ranch, 271, 272
Doheny Road, 275
Dolores' Drive-In, 259
Domaleche, Bernart, 19
Downey, John G., 17
Dozier, William, 361
Drury Lane, 275

Drought, 15, 22
Dunhill, Alfred, 341
Durante, Jimmy, 158, 301

Edwards, Blake, 303
"El Camino Real", 332
Eldridge, Florence, 304
Elm Drive, 94, 180
El Rodeo de las Aguas, 114
El Rodeo School, 114, 115, 161
Eucalyptus tree, 17, 19
Executive Life Insurance company, 367

Fairbanks, Douglas, 63, 70, 96, 113,
    158, 375
Fairchild's Restaurant, 258
Fiftieth Anniversary, 296, 298, 299
First Church of Christ, Scientist, 216
Flewelling, Ralph, 185
Flower shows, 54
Foothill, Road, 322, 326
Forbes, Ralph, 87
The Forties, 226
Fox Studios, 116, 163
Francis-Orr Stationery, 135
Frank, Abe, 174
Franklin Canyon reservoir, 199
Frascati Inn, 259
Friars Club of California, Inc., 316
Friars Club Charity Foundation, 316
Friends of the Library, 90

Gable and Lombard, 354
Gage, Merrill, 185
Garland, Judy, 263
Gateway Lodge, 329
Glendale Federal Savings, 371
Goddard, Paulette, 230
Goetz, Milton, 72
Goldwyn, Sam, 83
Gone With The Wind, 325
Gonzales, "Pancho", 288
Goodyear blimp, 119
Gorme, Edie, 361
Grauman, Sid, 174
Great Drepression, 163, 164, 201, 206
Great Western Savings Center, 233,
    373
Green, Burton E., 23, 24, 26, 48, 72,
    354
Green, Johnny, 302
Greenacres, 138-151, 199

Grey, Amelia, 314
Greystone, 124-133, 271, 272
Griffith, Corinne, 71, 87, 246
Gucci, 314
Guggenheim, Mrs. Carrie, 153
Gwendolyn Drive, 42

Haddock, Lon, 204
Hahn, Sam, 103
Hamilton Drive, 233
Hamilton, Joe, 358
Hammel, Henry, 22
Hammell & Denker Ranch, 17, 19, 21,
    23
Hammett, Dashiel, 83
Hancock, Major Henry, 14, 15
Harlow, Jean, 209
Harris, Phil, 158
Harrison, Rex, 291
Hartford Way, 354
Hawthorne Grammar School, 52, 94,
    114, 161, 374
Hayworth, Rita, 293
Hearst, Fannie, 83
Heifetz, Jasha, 83
Hellman, Irving, 50, 72, 169
Hepburn, Katharine, 353
Hermes, 340
Hillel Hebrew Academy, 255
Hillcrest Road, 275
Hilton, Conrad, 253, 264, 269
Hollywood, 282, 318
Hongkong Bank of California, 372
Horace Mann School, 161
Horse shows, 96
Hotel Hollywood, 30, 31, 35
Hughes, Howard, 226
Hunter and Hounds, 93

Ince, Thomas H., 83, 88
Indian raids, 14
Indianapolis 500, 56

Jacquemart, Henri Alfred Marie, 93
Jax, 314
Johnson, Kirk B., 49
Jolson, Al, 177
Jones, Bobby, 193
Juel Park, 260
Jurgenson's, 256

Kahn, Ali, 293

Keaton, Buster, 83
Keeler, Ruby, 177
Kelly, Gene, 361
Kenyon, Doris, 262
Kerckhoff, William G., 23, 103
Kerckhoff, Mrs. William G., 103
Kerckhoff Hall, 103
King Gillette, 42
Kirkeby, Arnold S. 288
KJOI Radio, 238
Klein, Eugene V., 48
Klein, Frances, 314
KMPC Radio, 238
Kraley, Hans, 86
Kreiss, Milton F., 288

LaBallona Creek, 9
LaBallona, town of, 23
LaCienega Boulevard, 19, 123, 320
LaCienega Park, 188
Laemmle, Carl, 83
Lamour, Dorothy, 158
La Scala, 344
Lawn Bowling Club, 190
Lawrence, Steve, 361
Lawry's Restaurant, 258
Lee, Peggy, 158
Levant, Oscar, 304
Lewis, George, 153
Lewis Station, 44
Lexington Road, 24, 48, 246, 331,
    339, 354
Linden Drive, 171
Little Santa Monica Boulevard, 26, 81,
    157, 172, 316
Litton Industries. 322-326
Litton Plaza, 322-327
Livingston, Mary, 303
Lloyd, Harold, 70, 138, 158, 185, 298
Lloyd, Mrs. Elizabeth Fraser, 185
Lomitas, 27
London Shop, 235
Longyear, W.D., 93
Loper, Don, 261
Los Angeles, 8, 11, 14, 22, 23, 26, 47,
    52, 68, 102, 113, 124, 163, 164, 255,
    285, 318
—Athletic Club, 22
—Avenue, 22
—City Council, 13
—County Flood Control District, 187,
    190

—County Library, 301
—Country Club, 114
—Riding Club, 96
—School Board, 116
Luau, 256
Lubitch, Ernst, 86, 169
Luckman, Charles, 335
Luft, Lorna, 362

MacArthur, Charles, 83
MacDonald, Jeannette, 83
Magnin, I., 234
Main Street, 14, 22
Manufacturers Bank Building, 367
The Man With The Golden Arm, 263
Maple Drive, 180, 197, 318
March, Fredric, 304
Margaret Herrick Library, 363
Marina del Rey, 23
Market Street, 22
Marquis Theater, 164, 363
Mayer, Louis B., 83
McCarty, Walter G., 61, 96, 154, 246,
    288
McGuire, Dorothy, 358
McHugh, Jimmy, 226, 299
Mellon, Andrew, 204
Melody Lane Restaurant, 259
Melrose Avenue, 363
Metro-Goldwyn-Mayer, 238
Mexico, 8, 10, 310
Millard, Mrs. Jay B., 91
Miller, Roger, 362
Minnelli, Liza, 362
Minnelli, Vincent, 301
Mitchell, Thomas, 231
Mix, Tom, 70, 83, 158, 176
Montez, Maria, 230
Moorehead, Agnes, 291
Morgan, Frank, 298
Morocco Junction, 22, 23, 68
Mount Calvary Lutheran Church, 227
Mount Wilson, 14
Mudd, Harvey, 211
Murphy, George, 304
Murphy, Jimmy, 61
Music Corporation of America, 325
Myers, Ben, 72

Nadeau, Remi, 17, 22
Nagle, Conrad, 70, 83, 298
Nate 'n Al, 344

National Editorial Association, 54
National General Corporation, 48
Negri, Pola, 83
Newman, Paul, 356
Niblo, Fred, 70, 83, 262, 298

Ocean Park Speedway, 56
Olympic Boulevard, 58, 71, 123, 213, 255, 339
Our Lady the Queen of the Angels of Porciuncúla, 8

Pacific Electric, 26, 72, 194, 285
Pacific Electric Station, 29, 48, 52, 68
Palos Verdes, 15
Panamint mines, 22
Park Way, 39, 44
Parker, Dorothy, 83
Parsons, Louella, 83
Pasadena, 14
Peck and Caufield, 56
Perpetual Savings & Loan Association, 369
Pesterre's, 135
Peters, Jon, 341
Pickfair, 63-65, 83
Pickford, Mary, 63, 65, 70, 158, 163, 169
Pico Boulevard, 17, 19, 58, 246
Pioneer Oil Company, 17
The Point, 156, 193, 253
Polo, Ralph, 341
Polo Lounge and Patio, 202, 348, 352
Portola, Captain Don Gaspar de, 8, 9
Powell, Dick, 158
Powell, William, 246
Preuss, Edward A., 17, 19
Preuss Road, 17, 58, 96

Queen Juliana, 351

Rabbi Harrison Chapel, 220
Rainier, Prince and Princess, 351
Rancho LaBrea, 14, 17
Reeder, W.A., 42
Residences, 27, 48-51, 82-88, 124-133, 138-153, 207-211, 230-231, 280-281, 290-295, 300-305, 310, 356-361
—Gracie Allen, 295
—Julie Andrews, 303
—Lucille Ball, 360
—Theda Bara, 84
—John Barrymore, 85
—Wallace Beery, 207
—Jack Benny, 303
—Edgar Bergen, 295
—Francis V. Betiller, 153
—Roland P. Bishop, 50
—Fred Brisson, 301
—Carol Burnett, 358
—George Burns, 295
—Charles Chaplin, 84
—Ruth Chatterton, 87
—Henry C. Clark, 27
—Harry Cohn, 230
—Ronald Colman, 295
—Olivia deHavilland, 230
—Edward Doheny, Jr., 124
—William Dozier, 361
—Jimmy Durante, 301
—Blake Edwards, 303
—Florence Eldrige, 304
—Douglas Fairbanks, 62
—Ralph Forbes, 87
—Paulette Goddard, 230
—Edie Gorme, 361
—Burton Green, 48
—Johnny Green, 302
—Corinne Griffith, 87
—Carrie Guggenheim, 153
—Joe Hamilton, 358
—Jean Harlow, 209
—Rex Harrison, 291
—Rita Hayworth, 293
—Thomas Ince, 88
—Kirk B. Johnson, 49
—Ali Kahn, 293
—Gene Kelly, 361
—Eugene V. Klein, 48
—Hans Kraley, 86
—Steve Lawrence, 361
—Oscar Levant, 304
—George Lewis, 153
—Mary Livingston, 303
—Harold Lloyd, 138
—Fredric March, 304
—Dorothy McGuire, 358
—Vincent Minnelli, 301
—Tom Mix, 83
—Maria Montez, 230
—Agnes Moorehead, 291
—Gary Morton, 360
—George Murphy, 304
—Paul Newman, 356
—Mary Pickford, 62
—Debbie Reynolds, 357
—Edward G. Robinson, 305
—Virginia Robinson, 210
—Charles "Buddy" Rogers, 64
—Will Rogers, 83
—Michael Romanoff, 230
—James Roosevelt, 294
—Rosalind Russell, 301
—Ann Rutherford, 361
—Dinah Shore, 357
—Phil Silvers, 304
—Jimmy Stewart, 359
—Gloria Swanson, 89
—Norma Talmadge, 84
—Elizabeth Taylor, 290
—Michael Todd, 290
—Lana Turner, 292
—Ben Turpin, 87
—Rudolph Valentino, 82
—Lupe Valez, 208
—Conrad Veidt, 84
—Clifton Webb, 295
—Max Whittier, 50
—Joanne Woodward, 356
Restaurant Row, 258
Rexford Drive, 42, 52, 216, 307
Reynolds, Debbie, 357
Richlor's Restaurant, 258
Riggs, Bobby, 288
River Porciuncúla, 8
Riverside, 14
Robertson Boulevard, 17, 19, 58, 96, 103, 240
Robinson, Edward G., 305
Robinson, Mrs. Virginia, 210, 299
Robinson's Beverly, 156, 210, 236, 253
Rocha, Jose Antonio, 17
Roches, Antonio, adobe, 19
Rodeo de las Aguas, 13, 17, 375
Rodeo Drive, 26, 39, 42, 72, 73, 105, 116, 174, 240, 253, 260, 296, 316, 362
Rodeo Land & Water Company, 23, 30, 47, 70, 72, 105
Rodeos, 15
Rogers, Charles "Buddy", 65
Rogers, Will, 63, 70, 72, 83, 97, 113, 163, 202, 204, 214
Roland, Ruth, 96
Romanoff, Michael, 230, 240
Romanoff's Restaurant, 240, 316
Roosevelt, Franklin D., 206
Roosevelt, James, 295
Round-the-World flyers, 54
Roxbury Drive, 96
Roxbury Park, 190
Rubinstein, Arturo, 83
Russell, Rosalind, 301
Rutherford, Ann, 361

Saint-Germain, 341
Saks Fifth Avenue, 164, 212, 235
The Saloon, 345
San Antonio, 13
Santa Barbara, 17
Santa Barbara Company, 11
San Diego, 8
San Diego Chargers, 48
San Gabriel, 11
Santa Maria, 22
Santa Monica, 23, 54, 56, 68, 102
—Bay, 124
—Boulevard, 26, 28, 39, 42, 47, 72, 74, 76, 93, 105, 106, 108, 156, 159, 164, 169, 179, 181, 185, 193, 206, 264, 313, 317, 318
—Mountains, 30, 271
—Park, 179
Sarnez Restaurant, 259
Sassoon, 340
Scholarship Loan Fund, 90
Script, 214
Segura, "Pancho", 288
Senior Citizen Center, 190
Serra, Father Junipero, 8
The Seventies, 328
Sharp, Evelyn, 288
Sherman, town of, 14, 42, 123
Shore, Dinah, 158, 357
Shriners, 54
Silberstein, Ben, 348
Sills, Milton, 262
Silver Anniversary, 298
Silvers, Phil, 304
Sinatra, Frank, 263
Sister City Program, 310
The Sisters of the Holy Cross, 171
The Sixties, 296
Skelton, Red, 158
Sloane, W. & J., 235
Smith, Martha, 218
Soldiers' Home, Sawtelle, 56
Sonoma, 10

Spalding, Silsby, 72
"Spirit of Beverly Hills" flying
  fortress, 229
Spring of the Sycamores of St.
  Stephen, 9
Stein, Jules, 325
Stewart, Jimmy, 359
Street sign, 248
Sunset Boulevard, 13, 23, 27, 28, 50,
  72, 73, 90, 96, 156, 248, 310, 329,
  346
Sunset Park, 37, 42, 251
Sunset, town of, 23
Swall Drive, 100
Swanson, Gloria, 42, 83, 89, 248
Swiss Cafe, 261

Talmadge, Constance, 83
Talmadge, Norma, 83, 84
Tanner Motor Tours, 89
Tar pits, 14
Taylor, Elizabeth, 291
Temple, Francis P.F., 22
Temple Emanuel, 220-225
Temple Street, 14
The Thirties, 164
Thomas, Danny, 158
Thompson, Kay, 288
Tiffany's, 314
Time, Life & Fortune, 246
Todd, Michael, 291
Tomlin, Lily, 362
Tournament of Roses, 121
Tower Road, 80
Trade at Home Week, 54
Trader Vic's Restaurant, 266
Treaty of Guadalupe Hidalgo, 10
Trenton Drive, 181
"The Triangle", 164, 246
Trousdale Estates, 271-282
Turner, Lana, 292
Turpin, Ben, 87
The Twenties, 54

UCLA, 102, 103
Uncle Bernie's Toy Menagerie, 261
Union-Hollywood Water Company,
  123
United California Bank, 368
United States Hotel, 22
Universal Pictures, 354

Valdez, Eugenio, 10,11
Valdez, Luciano, 13,14
Valdez, Maria Rita, 11, 13, 14, 17
Valentino, Rudolph, 54, 70, 82, 83
Valez, Lupe, 208
Van Cleef & Arpels, 340
Veidt, Conrad, 84
Venice, town of, 102
Victor Hugo Restaurant, 219, 236
Victory gardens, 226
Villa, Mariano, 17
Villa, Vicente Ferrer, 10, 11
Volpe, Nicholas, 177

Wadsworth, Ralph D., 116
Wagner, Rob, 214
Wanger, Walter, 202
War bond drives, 226, 229
Warner's Beverly, 193
Washington, Ned, 299
Webb, Clifton, 295
Wellborn, Judge Olin, 24
Wellborn, Lilian, 24
Werlé, 341
West Adams Boulevard, 26
West Adams Community School, 255
Western Avenue, 100
West Hollywood, 14, 123, 164, 363
West Los Angeles, 9
Westwood, 14, 23, 102
Whittier Drive, 114, 226, 346
Whittier Max, 23, 48, 50, 72
Whitworth, James, 19
Whitworth Ranch, 17, 19
William Morris Agency, 321
Williams, Andy, 362
Williams Brothers, 288
Will Rogers Park, 251
Wilshire Boulevard, 8, 22, 26, 28, 56,
  58, 74, 114, 156, 159, 164, 172, 174,
  185, 193, 212, 226, 233, 236, 240,
  256, 264, 288, 308, 313, 317, 318,
  320, 363, 364
Wilson, Benjamin Davis, 14, 17, 19,
  375
Windsor, Duke and Duchess, 246, 351
Wodehouse, P.G., 83
"Wonderful World of Beverly Hills",
  299
Woods, Charles, 103
Woodward, Joanne, 356

Workman, William, 15, 375
WPA workers, 164
Wright, Frank Lloyd, 253

Ye Bridle Path, 72, 73
Ye Little Club, 256
YMCA, 248
Young, Robert, 298
Yvel, 260

Zanuck, Darryl, 202